THINK HISTORY! 3

MODERN TIMES
1750–1990

Caro... ...r Clive Griffiths Amanda Jacob

S... editor: Lindsay von Elbing

heinemann.co.uk

✓ Free online support
✓ Useful weblinks
✓ 24 hour online ordering

01865 888080

Inspiring generations

Heinemann is an imprint of Pearson Education Limited,
a company incorporated in England and Wales, having
its registered ocffice at Edinburgh Gate, Harlow, Essex,
CM20 2JE. Registered company number: 872828

Heinemann is a registered trademark of Pearson Education Limited

© Caroline Beechener, Clive Griffiths, Amanda Jacob, 2004

First published 2004

09 08
10 9

British Library Cataloguing in Publication Data is available from the British Library
on request.

ISBN 978 0 435 31370 8

Copyright notice

Designed, illustrated and typeset by IFA Design Ltd, Plymouth, Devon
Original illustrations © Pearson Education Limited 2003
Printed and bound in China (CTPS/09)

Photographic acknowledgements

The authors and publisher would like to thank the following for permission to reproduce
photographs:
AKG, pages 141 (left), 157 (right) 158 (left and right); AP Photo, pages 101 (right), 103, 190
(right); Art Archive, pages 17, 22, 23 (bottom), 176, 213 (top); Associated Press, page 105;
Bilderdienst Suddeutscher Verlag, page 129 (top); Bodleian Library, page 119; Bridgeman/
Manchester City Art Galleries, page 64; Commonwealth War Grave Commission, page 114;
Corbis, pages 104, 108, 148 (bottom right); Corbis/Bettman, page 100; Corbis/Harcourt
Index, page 148 (bottom left); Corbis/Richard T. Nowitz, page 145 (right); Deutsches
Historisches Museum Berlin, page 126 (left); Fotomas Index, pages 29; Freemantle Media,
page 45; Hulton Archive, pages 7 (bottom), 15, 21, 23 (top), 24 (top and bottom), 30, 42, 52,
57, 71, (top), 79 (top right, bottom left), 85, 89, 93 (top), 99 (top and bottom), 111, 118, 120
(bottom), 152, 204, 206 (top and bottom), 207 (top and bottom), 216 (right); Ronald Grant
Archive, page 145, (top left); Illustrated London News, page 179; Imperial War Museum,
pages 192 (left and middle), 196; Katz Pictures, page 209 (left); Mansell Collection, page 48;
Mary Evans Picture Library, pages 4, 7 (top), 27, 53, 71 (bottom), 79 (middle, bottom right),
120 (top) 138, 157, (left), 214; PA Photos, page 218; Peter Newark's American Pictures,
pages 79 (top left), 88, 93 (bottom), 102, 192 (right); Popperfoto, pages 144, 208, 209 (right);
Public Record Office Image Library, pages 203 (top and bottom right), 216 (left); Punch,
pages 5, 20, 73, 170; Schomburg Center for Research in Black Culture, New York, page 98;
Science and Society, page 43; The Sternberg Centre, page 145 (bottom left); Topham
Picturepoint, pages 74, 75, 101 (left), 141 (right), 177; University of Kent Centre for the
Study of Cartoons and Caricatures, pages 189, 190 (bottom left); USHMM, courtesy of R.
Harrison, page 142; USHMM Photo Archives, page 126 (right); Weiner Archive, pages 135,
140; Zydowski Institute, page 134; Source unknown, pages 55, 129 (bottom), page 148
(top), 163, 167, 190 (top left), 195, 201 (both), 213 (bottom), 215.

Cover photograph: 'Search lights in the night sky' from the Occupation Triptych, 1990, by
Derek Crow, © the Bridgeman Art Library/Jersey Museum

Picture research by Frances Topp

Written source acknowledgements

The publishers have made every effort to contact copyright holders. However, if any
material has been incorrectly acknowledged, the publishers would be pleased to correct
this at the earliest opportunity.

CONTENTS

THEME: REVOLUTIONS

INTRODUCTION

WAS 1750 TO 1900 AN ERA OF PROGRESS?

In your study of history so far you may have learned about political revolutions – in England and America. This chapter is also about revolutions – but they are revolutions that have had an impact on everyday life.

On 1 May 1851, the Great Exhibition was opened in London by Queen Victoria. It brought together thousands of exhibits, with more than half of them being British. Approximately six million visitors came – many of them ordinary workers. The aim was to celebrate the progress being made in science, the arts and technology. The exhibition also intended to show everyone that Britain was the leading industrial nation – the 'workshop of the world'. The organisers, including Prince Albert (Queen Victoria's husband), felt that Britain had made great progress in the nineteenth century. But did everyone feel the same way? Look at Sources A and B, which are about the Great Exhibition.

SOURCE A

A contemporary engraving showing some of the exhibits at the Great Exhibition in 1851.

A Punch cartoon from 1852 showing specimens from Mr Punch's industrial exhibition of 1850.

💡 What different impressions of the Great Exhibition do you think are given by Sources A and B?

💡 Why do you think the artists wanted to create this impression? Share your ideas with the rest of the class.

This was certainly an age of great change, but was it an age of progress? You will decide as you work through this section.

1

WERE THE CHANGES IN AGRICULTURE A REVOLUTION?

WHAT CHANGES TOOK PLACE IN FARMING AFTER 1700?

Objectives

In this section you will find out:
- how land was enclosed after 1700
- why land was enclosed after 1700.

To investigate these ideas you will:
- assess a range of sources that outline the two systems of farming
- write a speech about the advantages and disadvantages of land enclosure

Starter

Take a look at the bar chart and Sources A to D. Then brainstorm the questions that follow.

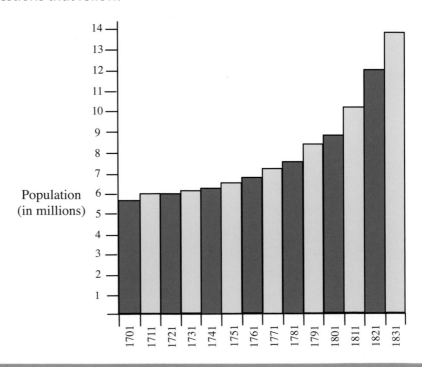

Bar chart showing the rising population in Britain, 1700–1830.

SOURCE A

A contemporary view of the city of Manchester in 1850.

SOURCE B

A contemporary picture showing farming by hand in the nineteenth century.

SOURCE C

One man has an acre of land divided into eight strips with each strip set apart over a large common field.

A description of farming methods in 1794.

SOURCE D

Key words

Scab This word is used here to mean a skin disease caused by small insects.

If any part of the flock had the **scab** or other infectious disease, there was no means of stopping it from spreading.

From a report on farming in 1794.

💡 Why do you think there was a growing demand for food in the nineteenth century?

💡 Why do you think existing farming practices might be unable to meet this demand? Share your ideas with the rest of the class.

What was farming like in 1700?

In 1700 the system of farming used in many parts of England had changed very little since the Middle Ages. Villages were usually surrounded by large, unfenced fields. These fields were divided into narrow strips. Each farmer would either own or rent a number of strips scattered across the three fields. This was known as the open-field system of farming. Some farmers would have to travel two or three miles to visit all their strips of land.

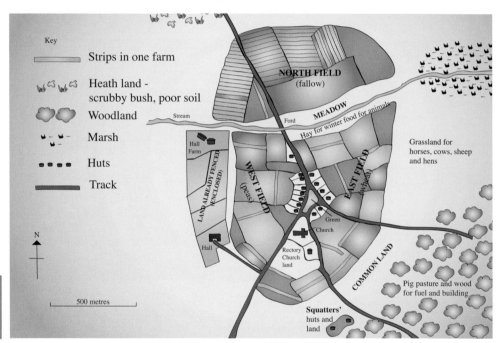

The open-field system of farming.

Farmers co-operated with one another, to decide which crops would be grown in the fields. A simple system of crop rotation was used. This was known as the three course rotation.

Three course rotation

Every year, two fields were sown with crops. The third was left **fallow**. Animals could graze on the stubble and weeds in the fallow land, and their manure fertilised the soil. Any changes to the three course rotation had to be agreed by all the farmers in the village. Villagers had the right to graze their cattle and sheep on **the common**. This meant that animals belonging to all the farmers would mix together. Villagers also had the right to take timber from the woodland.

💡 What difficulties do you think a farmer would face if he wanted to grow alternative (different) crops on his strips or improve the quality of his animals?

Key words

Fallow Land left unsown or unploughed for a time.

The common Land that all the villagers could use.

What main changes took place in farming after 1700?

The need for greater supplies of food for a growing population meant that farming needed to change. The big change in agriculture that allowed all the others to happen was known as 'enclosure'. This involved combining farmers' strips of land into larger blocks and surrounding them with hedges, walls or fences. Most of the common land was also enclosed and people lost their right to cut timber from woodland.

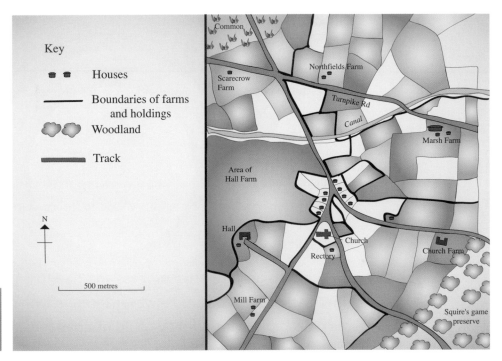

The enclosed-field system of farming.

Enclosure was not a new idea. By 1700 many open fields had already been enclosed. As a result, some farmers had become richer than others – enclosed fields were generally more productive than open fields. This process of enclosing land increased from 1750. By the middle of the nineteenth century, almost all the open fields had disappeared.

How was land enclosed?

The best way for enclosure to happen was by the agreement of all the villagers. But it could also be forced through by law if the holders of 80 per cent of the land agreed.

Those who wanted the land to be enclosed had to inform all the villagers of their plans. A notice had to be posted on the village church door.

Parliament was then asked to pass an Enclosure Act for the village.

Enclosure commissioners were sent to the village to survey the open fields, examine documents and hear the claims of the villagers. This was supposed to make sure that everyone in the village who was legally entitled to land got their fair share.

The commissioners awarded blocks of land to the farmers. Some got better land than others.

Each farmer then planted hedges around his land, dug ditches and built a farm house on his plot. Roads were also built from the village to the new farms.

Enclosure was an expensive process and had to be paid for by the farmers who received land. However, farmers who received small plots of land often found they could not pay the costs and were forced to sell their plots to richer farmers.

The enclosure of land – for better or worse?

TASKS...

1 Read the list of statements on page 11. Some support enclosure and some oppose it.

On a chart like the one below, note down the numbers of the statements that support enclosure. Then note down the numbers of the statements that oppose it. **WS**

Statements that support enclosure	Statements that oppose enclosure

1 We all have a fair share of good and bad land.

2 We waste too much time travelling between our strips. Compact farms will save time.

3 The strips are too small to make it worthwhile using new tools such as the seed drill.

4 We are self-sufficient, which means we grow our own food and rear our own livestock.

5 Weeds from strips belonging to lazy farmers have spread to our land.

6 We will be able to try new methods to increase the amount of food we produce without getting everyone's agreement.

7 Enclosure is expensive. Not everyone will be able to afford to pay for new fences, farmhouses and roads.

8 We will be able to breed healthier animals because our animals will no longer mix with diseased ones on the common. This will lead to more milk and meat being produced.

9 We will be deprived of our right to cut timber from the woodland and graze our animals on the common land.

10 We will have more land, because the common land, meadows, woodland and wasteland will be shared out.

11 There will be more people in the village who do not own land. This will lead to more poverty, because not everyone will be able to find jobs.

12 Too much land is left uncultivated each year. This is not very efficient.

13 Our way of life will change. The **hayward**, **swineherd** and **pinder** will lose their jobs.

14 We could improve our land by draining it. More land could then be farmed.

Key words

Hayward Someone who looked after the meadows.

Swineherd Someone who looked after the villagers' pigs.

Pinder Someone who rounded up stray cattle.

TASKS...

1 Imagine you live in a village in 1780. The villagers decide to hold a meeting to discuss whether all the open fields should be enclosed.

a) Look at the two sides of the argument presented by the **freeholder** and the **yeoman**.

> I have four strips scattered over three main fields. Two of my strips are on poor land. This affects the amount of food I can grow. As well as farming my own strips, I have to take any labouring jobs going to make ends meet. I keep geese and chickens on the common. Enclosing the land in the village would mean a lot of extra work building fences in the short term. But I could not afford the legal costs or pay to have my land fenced off ... if I get any. I no longer have the documents to prove my legal rights to the land I farm.

A poor freeholder.

> I have twelve strips scattered over three fields. I know there is money to be made in the new farming methods and I am keen to try them. I want to grow vegetables rather than wheat and barley. But I'm frustrated because not everyone in the village agrees with my ideas. I want to try selective breeding, but there is no point because my animals will get mixed up on the common with other people's.

A wealthy yeoman.

b) Now use the statements you sorted on page 11 to complete a speech for either the freeholder or the yeoman. The purpose of your speech is to persuade people to agree with your view about enclosure.

Guidelines are provided on page 13, to help you with this piece of writing. **WS**

Key words

Freeholder Someone who owned or rented a small amount of land in the village.

Yeoman Someone who was a wealthy landowner.

Selective breeding Choosing only the best animals to breed from.

TASKS...

Tips for writing your speech

- Begin with a powerful opening statement about why you think your view should be chosen. Put forward each of the main arguments supporting your view. Back up each one with evidence. Then explain why the opposite view should not be adopted. End your speech with a conclusion in which you repeat the main arguments for supporting your view.
- Write your speech in the first person and the present tense. Use connectives that are related to logic such as *in fact, because, therefore, however*.
- Use words that will influence others in the village such as *obviously, importantly, clearly, surely, undoubtedly*.

Plenary

Study the following charts, which are for the village of Aldsworth in Gloucestershire.

	Before enclosure	After enclosure
Acres of land sown with wheat	200	390
Acres of land sown with barley	200	390
Acres of land sown with oats and peas	300	390
Total acreage under cultivation	700	1170
Sheep bred each year	200	1800

	Before enclosure	After enclosure
Amount of wheat produced	150 **quarters**	585 quarters
Amount of barley produced	250 quarters	825 quarters
Amount of oats and peas produced	320 quarters	950 quarters
Total amount of crops grown	720 quarters	2360 quarters
Number of fleeces per **tod**	8	5

Key words

Acre A measure of land (about 4 kilometres square).

Quarter A grain measure of 8 bushels (about 13 kilograms).

Tod A weight of wool (about 13 kilograms).

- What were the main results of enclosure for Aldsworth?
- How would landowners have benefited from enclosure?
- How would the general public benefit from enclosure?
- Do you think that enclosure was justified? Explain your answer.

Discuss your answers with others in your class.

WHAT WERE THE EFFECTS OF ENCLOSURE?

Objectives

In this section you will find out:
- how enclosure led to other changes in farming methods in the eighteenth and nineteenth centuries
- the effects of those changes.

To investigate these ideas you will:
- assess the benefits and drawbacks of changes in farming in the eighteenth and nineteeth centuries
- reach an informed decision on whether the changes in agriculture can be called a revolution.

Starter

Read Source A.

1771: In the **vale** of Evesham the average fleece is 9 pounds (4 kilograms) in the enclosures, but only 3 pounds (1.35 kilograms) in the open fields. By enclosing, one sheep yields as much as three used to.

1774: Several men in enclosed counties are constantly employed in winter hedging and ditching. What comparison can there be between the open-field system of a half or a third of the lands being in fallow, with a scarcity of employment?

1801: After giving me an account of 20 enclosures for which he had acted as a commissioner, Mr Foster **lamented** that he had been partly responsible for **injuring** 2000 poor people at the rate of 20 families per parish. The poor are injured by 19 out of 20 Enclosure Acts. The poor in these parishes may say, and with truth, 'All I know is I had a cow, and an Act of Parliament has taken it from me.'

1813: From Lincoln to Barton, all – or very nearly all – of the land was **heath**. But now it is enclosed by Acts of Parliament. The result has been that the tenants live much better and show in every circumstance signs of greater prosperity.

The records of a farmer, Arthur Young, from 1771 to 1813.

Key words

Vale Valley.
Lament To express regret or sadness.
Injure To make worse off.
Heath Barren open land.

💡 *What do you think were the advantages and disadvantages of enclosure according to Arthur Young?*

💡 *Can you think of any reasons why Arthur Young could say such different things about the effects of enclosure? Discuss these reasons with other people in your class.*

How did enclosure lead to an increase in agricultural production?

Once land had been enclosed, some farmers were able to experiment with new machinery, crops, methods of cultivation, fertilisers and selective breeding. These new methods led to an increase in agricultural production.

New machines

In 1701 Jethro Tull invented the seed drill, which sowed seeds in straight rows and covered them up with earth afterwards. Before this, seeds had been sown by hand. The enclosure of farmland led to this invention being more widely used in the nineteenth century.

SOURCE B

A painting of 1720 of the inventor, Jethro Tull.

☀ Why do you think that enclosure led to the seed drill being more widely used?

Key words

Threshing Separating the wheat from the stalks it grows on.

Ploughs were also improved. An all-iron plough was developed in the early 1800s and in 1826 the first steam plough was developed. In 1786, the **threshing** machine was invented and its use became more common in the 1820s.

☀ Why do you think that enclosure led to new machines being more widely used?

☀ What effect do you think these new machines had on farm labourers?

New methods of cultivation

One of the most important changes in arable areas (areas where crops are grown) was four field crop rotation. Developed in Norfolk by Viscount Townshend, this method used barley, wheat, turnips and clover.

This new system helped to increase crop yields (the amount grown) because it eliminated the need to leave land lying fallow. The different crops used also kept the soil fertile, for example clover and turnips replaced the nutrients that wheat and barley used up.

Animals grazed on the fields of clover. As they ate, they added manure to the soil. Turnips and grasses such as clover also had the added benefit of increasing the amount of **fodder** crops that could be stored in winter and fed to animals. This meant that more animals could be kept over the winter months.

TASKS...

1 a) Copy these two diagrams into your exercise book.

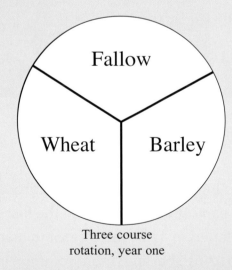

Three course rotation, year one

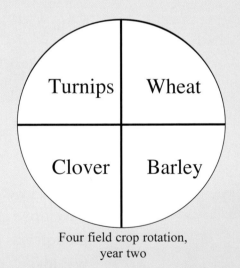

Four field crop rotation, year two

b) Complete the diagrams for years 2, 3 and 4 to show how each crop rotation system worked.

2 What do you think were the benefits of the four field crop rotation system? Explain your answer carefully.

New fertilisers

Fertilisers were used to enrich the soil and increase crop yields. Animal manure was the easiest fertiliser to use as it was readily available. But human waste from towns was also used. From the 1840s, artificial fertilisers made from chemicals were available.

After enclosure, some farmers used a method called marling to improve the quality of the soil. Chalk or lime was added to heavy clay soils and clay was added to light soils to make them easier to cultivate.

Selective breeding

After enclosure, many farmers began to improve the quality of farm animals through selective breeding – choosing only the best animals to breed from. One of the most famous selective breeders was Robert Bakewell. He managed to produce a new, larger sheep called the New Leicester which produced a high level of fatty meat. The results of selective breeding can be seen in Source C and the table below.

SOURCE C

A contemporary painting showing the results of selective breeding in the nineteenth century.

	1710	1790
Cattle	370lbs (168kg)	800lbs (363kg)
Calves	50lbs (23kg)	143lbs (65kg)
Sheep	28lbs (13kg)	80lbs (36kg)
Lambs	18lbs (8kg)	50lbs (23kg)

Average weight of animals sold at Smithfield Market in London, 1710–90.

1 **a)** Look at the table on page 17. Draw a graph to show the percentage increase in the weight of animals sold at Smithfield between 1710 and 1790.

   b) Which animal's weight increased most?

2 Apart from greater quantities of meat, what do you think are the other advantages of breeding larger animals?

Was enclosure good for everybody?

Enclosure led to wealth and prosperity for many landowners. However, it led to poverty and hardship for many villagers. Farmers lost their land if they could not provide legal documents to prove it was theirs. Those who did receive small plots of land could not afford the cost of enclosure and usually sold up to wealthier neighbours.

Cottagers – people who did not have strips to farm, and who earned a very low income by keeping animals on the common and doing odd jobs – were most affected. Many were evicted from their homes.

Life was made worse for many of a village's poorer inhabitants because they could not graze their animals on the common or collect timber from the woodlands. Enclosure led to a 'social revolution' as many labourers were forced to leave their villages to go and work in the new factories in towns which offered the chance of better paid jobs and better living standards.

TASKS...

1 Could enclosure have been done differently to reduce the poverty and hardship suffered by many villagers? Explain your answer.

2 'The benefits of increased production outweighed the disadvantages of poverty and hardship for some villagers.' Explain whether you agree or disagree with this view.

Continued developments in the nineteenth century

Farming continued to develop in the nineteenth century. Wars with France between 1793 and 1815 meant that landowners made large profits. A shortage of European wheat meant home produced wheat could be sold for high prices. After the wars ended in 1815, landowners persuaded Parliament to pass the Corn Laws to keep wheat prices artificially high. The Corn Laws remained in place until 1846.

New technology, artificial fertilisers and new methods of drainage made farming more efficient and profitable whilst the development of railways meant landowners could sell their produce across the country. Towards the end of the century a series of poor harvests, outbreaks of animal diseases such as foot and mouth and cheap foreign imports from America, Australia and New Zealand affected the profits landowners were making.

Agricultural labourers fared less well. The French Wars and the Corn Laws led to high bread prices. This caused hardship and distress as bread was an important part of their diet. As farming became more efficient, many labourers faced unemployment and falling wages because fewer workers were needed to farm the land. Desperate farm labourers resorted to occasional acts of **sabotage** and **arson**. The most famous of these occurred in 1830 when there was an outbreak of rioting in the southern counties of England, known as the Swing Riots (see Chapter 3, pages 41–8).

Key words

Sabotage The destruction of an employer's property, such as tools or materials, by workers.

Arson Deliberately and illegally setting fire to property.

Many agricultural labourers left rural areas in search of work in the industrial towns and cities. This changed the balance of the population between the towns and countryside. In 1801, 69 per cent of the population lived in the countryside. By 1881 this had fallen to 32 per cent.

 What methods used by farmers today cause controversy? Explain why they cause such controversy.

TASKS...

1 A revolution is a complete change, often a sudden event leading to dramatic changes. Do you think the changes in agriculture were a 'revolution'? Give reasons for your answer.
   Use the following advice to help you give a good written answer. Write in the third person. **WS**

Introduction
Briefly state the issue. Explain that the changes in agriculture have been called a 'revolution' and that the purpose of your answer is to decide whether this is an accurate explanation of the changes that occurred.

Paragraph one
Explain why it is possible to argue that the changes in agriculture were a 'revolution'. Use quotes to support the points you make. Use connectives related to logic – *however, for example, as a result, clearly*.

TASKS...

Paragraph two

Explain why it is possible to argue that the changes in agriculture were not a 'revolution'. Use quotes to support the points you make. Use connectives related to logic – *however, for example, as a result, clearly*.

Conclusion

Comment on whether you think the changes in agriculture could be called a 'revolution', and why. Remember not to repeat yourself.

A *Punch* cartoon of 1844 called 'The Home of the Rick-burner'.

Plenary

Take a look at Source D. What do you think the man in the cartoon is being encouraged to do? What message do you think the artist wanted to give people about the hardship faced by farm labourers in the period after 1815? How do you think landowners would have responded to this cartoon? Explain your answer carefully.

2

WERE THE CHANGES IN INDUSTRY A REVOLUTION?

WHAT CHANGES TOOK PLACE IN THE COTTON TEXTILE INDUSTRY?

Objectives

In this section you will find out:
- the changes that took place in the cotton textile industry
- the impact these changes had on the production of cotton
- how machines changed the way people worked.

To investigate these ideas you will:
- assess how mechanisation improved productivity
- assess the impact of factories on the way people worked.

Starter

Take a look at Sources A and B.

SOURCE A

Spinning wool at home in the eighteenth century.

SOURCE B

Sixty years ago, cotton mills didn't exist. At present there are no fewer than 65. Most have been built during the present century. These mills, which are wholly involved in spinning cotton, are all worked by steam. The closeness of Oldham to Manchester, the great market for cotton goods, and good canals, but above all the abundant supply of coal from neighbouring towns, have made this one of the largest areas of **manufacture** in the country.

A description of Oldham by Edward Baines, 1825.

💡 *What changes do you think had taken place in the textile industry from Source A to Source B?*

💡 *How could the following have caused the changes the journalist Edward Baines is describing?*

- *Raw materials* • *Inventors* • *Improvements in farming*
- *Banks*   • *An empire* • *A rising population*

Key words

Manufacture The production of goods by machinery and on a large scale.

Britain was the first place in the world to have an **industrial revolution**. Between 1750 and 1900, British industry was very successful. By the middle of the nineteenth century, Britain was known as the 'workshop of the world'.

Industry is a huge topic. To help you understand the changes that took place and the impact of those changes, this section will concentrate on one industry – the textile industry.

Inventions in the textile industry

TASKS...

1   As you read through the following factfiles on inventions in the textile industry, on pages 22–4, complete a chart like the one below. **WS**

Invention	Inventor	Date of invention	Advantages of invention	Disadvantages of invention
	John Kay	1733		
Spinning Jenny	James Hargreaves			
Water Frame		1769		
	Samuel Crompton	1779		
Power loom	Edmund Cartwright			

factfile 1

Invention: The Flying Shuttle
Date: 1733
Inventor: John Kay of Bury, Lancashire
Power source: Hand power

The Flying Shuttle speeded up weaving, so more cloth could be woven. Only one weaver was now needed to weave on a broadloom. Fewer weavers were needed to make the same amount of cloth. Some weavers saw the Flying Shuttle as a threat to their jobs. The demand for spun cotton increased.

SOURCE **C**

The Flying Shuttle.

factfile 2

Invention: The Spinning Jenny
Date: 1767
Inventor: James Hargreaves of Blackburn, Lancashire
Power source: Hand power

The Spinning Jenny could be used in people's homes. A spinner using this could produce eight times more **yarn** than on a spinning wheel. It made a fine but weak thread. Spinners didn't like it because they saw it as a threat to their jobs. It balanced out the speed of spinning and weaving.

SOURCE D

A diagram of c. 1750 showing the Spinning Jenny.

Key words

Yarn Thread.

factfile 3

Invention: The Water Frame
Date: 1769
Inventor: Richard Arkwright of Preston, Lancashire
Power source: Water/steam power

The Water Frame made a strong and tough yarn. The yarn was coarse and not as fine as that made by the Spinning Jenny. It had to be put in a factory as it needed water to power it. It made spinning a much quicker process than weaving.

SOURCE E

A modern photograph of the Water Frame.

Invention: The Spinning Mule
Date: 1779
Inventor: Samuel Crompton of Bolton, Lancashire
Power source: Water/steam power

The Spinning Mule spun cotton on to 48 **spindles** at a time. It made a finer yarn than the water frame could make. The yarn it made was stronger than that made on the Spinning Jenny.

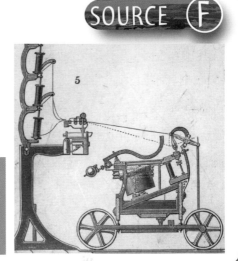

SOURCE F

A diagram from the time of the Spinning Mule.

Key words

Spindle A pin on a spinning machine used for twisting and winding the thread.

Invention: The Power Loom
Date: 1785
Inventor: Edmund Cartwright, a vicar from Leicestershire
Power source: Water/steam power

At first, it was difficult to get the Power Loom working properly. But William Horrocks and Richard Roberts made some improvements to the design in the early 1800s. Eventually, it speeded up weaving and helped mill owners to produce cloth of the same quality. It had to be used in a factory and, by the 1820s, thousands of handloom weavers lost their jobs.

SOURCE G

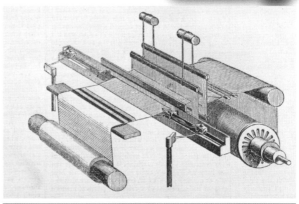

A diagram from the time of the Power Loom.

Year	Value of exports in £s
1710	5698
1751	45,986
1780	355,060
1800	5,406,501
	Cotton exports, 1710–1800.

TASKS...

1 Use the chart that you have filled in (see page 22) to help you decide which invention was the most influential in mechanising the cotton industry.

2 Imagine it is 1851. The Great Exhibition is being held to celebrate success in British industry. The organisers want to include the invention that was the most influential in mechanising the cotton industry. Write a letter to the organisers stating which invention they should include and why. The guidelines below will help you.

Purpose of the letter

To persuade people to agree that your choice of invention was the most influential in mechanising the cotton industry.

Letter layout

A formal letter. You will need an address, date, greeting (Dear Sirs) and closing (Yours faithfully).

What your letter should say

Begin with some powerful opening statements about the invention you think should be chosen. Back up each statement with evidence. Then explain why others should *not* be included in the exhibition.

How to end your letter

End with a conclusion in which you repeat the main arguments for including your choice of invention in the exhibition.

Sentence level

Write your letter in the first person and in the present tense. Use connectives that are related to logic such as *in fact, because, therefore*.

Word level

Use words that will influence the organisers of the Great Exhibition such as *obviously, importantly, clearly, surely, undoubtedly*.

3 Read the two historians' views on page 26. Sum up what each one thought.

4 *'The coming of factories changed people's working lives for the better.'*
Explain whether you agree or disagree with this statement.

How did the new machines change the way people worked?

Read the views of the two historians below.

Under the domestic system, spinners and weavers worked at home. They fixed their own working hours. Families worked together to produce the goods on simple small hand-operated machinery. Children would prepare the cotton for spinning, women would spin yarn and men would weave this into cloth.

They depended on the merchant to provide them with work. The merchant only paid the workers for what they made. He also fixed the workers' wages. Usually the workers rented the machines from the merchant. They had to pay rent on these machines even if there was no work. Often they owed the merchant money, which they borrowed when they were hard up.

Most of the workers lived in the countryside in small cottages. These cottages often had only one room downstairs. Cottages could be very cold, damp, draughty and dark during the winter. In summer, they were often hot and airless.

Working hours in the mills were long, often more than twelve hours a day. Exhaustion was a problem. Working in shifts was common.

The mills themselves were unhealthy places. They were full of extremely unpleasant smells – such as oil and grease. Cotton dust choked the workers' eyes and lungs. The mills were damp, humid and hot. They needed to be like this to stop the cotton yarn from breaking. The noise of the machines was deafening. The machines had no safety guards. Workers who lost or injured limbs were not paid if they were absent from work.

There were strict rules and harsh punishments. Workers were fined and beaten if they broke the rules. 'Strappers' were employed to beat children if they weren't working hard enough.

Children as young as seven worked long hours. Many became deformed from bending and crouching for long periods. Workers earned at least 25 per cent more than farm workers. As women and children could look after the machines, there was less work for men in the spinning mills.

Plenary

Did the changes in the textiles industry revolutionise the way people worked in the nineteenth century?

The last part of the twentieth century has been described as a 'technical revolution'. What do you think is meant by this phrase? How have these recent changes affected your life? Share your ideas with the rest of the class.

WERE FACTORIES REALLY THAT BAD?

Objectives

In this section you will find out:
- whether working conditions in factories were really that bad.

To investigate these ideas you will:
- use sources to find out about working conditions for children in the nineteenth century
- look at a range of interpretations of working conditions for children in the nineteeth century.

Starter

Look at Source A. It was drawn by a famous cartoonist, George Cruickshank, and it was published in 1816. When you study the cartoon it is important to realise that at this time there was no education for most children and it was expected that, by the age of about seven years old, children should be at work. This was not a new idea. Even before the development of factories, children helped their parents in the fields and in the home.

SOURCE A

An 1816 cartoon by George Cruickshank, commenting on the treatment of children working in factories.

What do you think is happening in Source A?

What message do you think George Cruickshank wanted to give about working conditions for children?

How useful do you think Source A is for finding out about the working conditions of children in the early nineteenth century?

To help them decide how useful a source is, historians need to know something about the person who wrote it. Read the information below, which tells you about the cartoon in Source A.

- *George Cruickshank was against children working in factories.*
- *Robert Peel was the politician chairing a committee investigating working conditions in 1816.*
- *Robert Peel was regarded as a sympathetic mill owner.*
- *It is unlikely that George Cruickshank ever visited Robert Peel's mill.*

💡 *Does this extra information lead you to change your first thoughts about the cartoon? If so, how and why?*

How factory owners treated their workers

When factories were being built towards the end of the eighteenth century, there were very few laws about working conditions. Factory owners could decide their own rules and regulations. Some factory owners took advantage of this. One criticism of many early factory owners was that they treated their workers, particularly women and children, very badly.

Some child workers were the sons and daughters of adult workers employed at the mill. Others were orphans, usually from large towns. Mill owners would agree to feed, clothe and house these children. They would live in a house near the mill.

Mill owners were keen to employ large numbers of children because they were paid less than adults. Also, they were more agile than adults. Some were used to 'scavenge' – that is, to crawl under the machines to clean away loose threads and dust. Others were used as 'piecers' to repair broken threads by joining the ends together. Mill owners paid **overlookers** to make sure the children worked hard. The more work the children did, the more the overlookers were paid.

Key words

Overlooker A person in charge of factory workers.

This picture comes from the book *The Adventures of Michael Armstrong, Factory Boy* by Francis Trollope, 1840. The story is about an orphan boy who started work at the age of six and was mistreated. It is based on the real life story of Robert Blincoe.

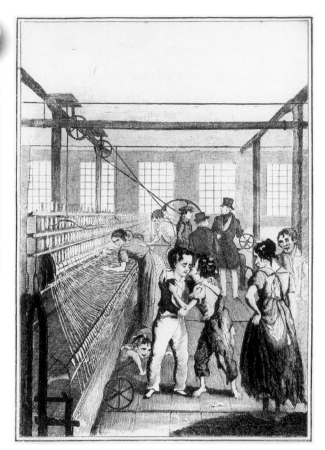

Once, two handles weighing a pound [0.5kg] each were screwed to my ears. Another time, three or four of us were made to hang from our hands above the machinery. Sometimes we had to stand up in a skip without our shirts on, and we were beaten with straps. Overlookers used to tie a 28 pound [about 14kg] weight to us and this hung down our backs.

Written by Robert Blincoe in 1828. He was an orphan who worked in the mills from an early age. His work made him deformed.

Question: Did working in the card-room affect your health?
Answer: Yes. It was so dusty. The dust got up my lungs, and the work was so hard. I got so bad in health, that when I pulled the baskets down, I pulled my bones out of their places.

An interview with Elizabeth Bentley in 1832. She worked as a child in the factories.

Interviews with hundreds of children were used in a number of reports about child labour. However, these reports were unlikely to be accurate because only the worst examples would have been included. Also, some factory reformers told witnesses to describe only the worst treatment.

Seventeen years ago a number of individuals, with myself, purchased the New Lanark establishment. There were 500 children. The hours at that time were thirteen a day. Their limbs were very generally deformed, their growth was stunted and they made very slow progress – even in learning the common alphabet. I came to the conclusion that the children were injured by being taken into the mills at this early age and employed for so many hours.

Written by Robert Owen, a mill owner, in 1816 to explain to Parliament why he did not employ children under the age of ten.

SOURCE F

Question: Have you observed that children in the factories have particular accidents?
Answer: Accidents were very often admitted to the infirmary, through the children's hands and arms having being caught in the machinery. In many instances the muscles and the skin is stripped down to the bone. In some instances a finger or two might be lost.

The observations of Dr Michael Ward in 1819.

From a book published in 1835. It was written by Edward Baines, a newspaper editor who defended mill owners and how they ran their mills.

SOURCE H

It is said that children are so cruelly beaten by the spinners or overlookers that their limbs become distorted and they grow up cripples. It is also said they are forced to work thirteen, fourteen or fifteen hours per day. This is the exception, not the rule. It is scarcely possible for any employment to be lighter [easier]. The position of the body is not harmful. The children walk about, and have the opportunity of frequently sitting if they feel like it. The minute fibres of cotton that float in the rooms are admitted, even by medical men, not to be harmful to young persons.

Written by Edward Baines in his newspaper, the Northern Mercury.

SOURCE I

Key words

Corporal punishment
Punishment through physical pain.

Apprentice Someone who is bound by a formal agreement to learn a trade or craft.

I have visited many factories and I never saw a single instance of **corporal punishment** inflicted on a child. The children seemed always to be cheerful and alert. The work of these lively elves seemed to resemble a sport. Conscious of their skill, they were delighted to show it off to any stranger. At the end of the day's work they showed no sign of being exhausted.

At Quarry Bank, near Wilmslow in Cheshire, stands a handsome house, built for the accommodation of the female **apprentices**. They are well fed, clothed and educated. The apprentices have milk-porridge for breakfast, potatoes and bacon for dinner, and meat on Sundays.

Written by Andrew Ure, a factory owner in 1835. Some employers like Ure believed that the factory system was good for workers.

SOURCE J

At the Bradford factory of Mr John Wood, workers looked healthy. Their hours of labour are not more than eleven each day. A surgeon is provided by the firm. If he notices anyone looking ill, he enquires about the cause. Should it be anything requiring rest or medicine, they are ordered home immediately. During the time they may be off work, their wages are sent to them, the same as if they had been at work.

Written by William Dodd, a former factory worker, in 1841.

TASKS...

1 Read the text on page 28 and take a good look at Sources B to J. Then, answer the following questions.

  a) Why do you think parents were keen to get their children jobs in cotton mills in the nineteenth century?

  b) In Source B, what impression do you think the illustration intended to convey?

  c) Pick out the words and phrases in Source E which show that Robert Owen was opposed to the use of children in mills.

  d) When do you think most accidents like the one described in Source F would occur? How could some accidents and injuries be avoided?

  e) Look at Source H. Pick out the words and phrases that show Baines supports the use of children in textile mills.

  f) Look at Source I. Why do you think Andrew Ure wanted to create this impression?

TASKS...

2 Imagine it is 1833. In small groups, you should produce *one* of the following.

- A leaflet for factory reformers who want to end child labour in factories. Your leaflet should put pressure on MPs to pass laws to end child labour, so it should concentrate on the very worst aspects of work in factories.

- A leaflet for factory owners who want to protect their right to use children in factories. Factory owners want you to concentrate on the very best examples of treatment in the factories. They have many supporters in Parliament, but want to make sure any laws passed do not restrict their rights to use children.

Use evidence from Sources B to J to help you with your leaflet. Sources B to F oppose child labour, Sources G to J support it.

You leaflet should include:

- an explanation of who the child workers are and why they are used in factories
- statements that support your chosen view of factory conditions for children
- statements from an expert who will question the reliability of the other side's evidence
- images to illustrate the points you are making
- a conclusion which has a catchy slogan to drive your message home.

3 Present your leaflets to the rest of the class. You could do this as an ICT presentation. After you have seen each other's presentations, evaluate your own leaflet.

For each of the questions below, think about the strengths of your work and things that could have been improved. **WS**

Content

Was the information included relevant? Did you give sufficient detail?

Presentation

Was the leaflet interesting? Did it include a mixture of writing and images? Did it engage the reader?

How persuasive was your leaflet?

Did your leaflet put forward a persuasive case for the point of view you adopted? Did you explain how the other point of view is unreliable?

How bad was the slavery in factories?

Thousands of our fellow creatures, both male and female, are now in a state of slavery. The streets are every morning wet by the tears of the innocent victims who are forced by the fear of the **strap** of the overlooker to hasten half-dressed to the **worsted** mills of Bradford. Thousands of little children from seven to fourteen years are daily forced to work from six in the morning to seven in the evening, with only 30 minutes for eating and recreation. Poor infants! You live in the boasted land of freedom and feel you are slaves.

A letter written by Richard Oastler to the Leeds Mercury. He wrote several letters under the heading of 'Yorkshire slavery' in the 1830s, comparing the working conditions of children in the mills to slavery in the British Empire.

Key words

Strap A leather belt used to beat children.

Worsted A type of woollen cloth.

In my recent tour of the factory districts I have seen tens of thousands of old, young and middle-aged men and women earning a good living in factories. They do their work without perspiring, protected from the summer sun and winter frost in bright, airy and healthy factory buildings. The power of steam has replaced the painful, muscular effort of the workers.

Written by Andrew Ure, a factory owner, in 1835.

TASKS...

Carefully read Sources K and L.

1 How do you think the views about the use of child labour differ?

2 Why do you think the writers have such different views about the use of child labour in textile mills in the early nineteenth century? Explain your answer carefully.

Did working conditions improve?

When laws were passed in 1802 and 1819 to reduce the hours of work for some children in cotton mills, they made little difference because the laws were not enforced. The activities of men like Robert Owen, Richard Oastler and Lord Shaftesbury persuaded Parliament to set up Royal Commissions to examine working conditions. These often resulted in the government introducing new laws to improve working conditions for men, women and children. The table shows some of the main laws passed to improve working conditions in mills.

1833	Children under the age of nine should not work at all. Children aged between nine and sixteen had their hours of work reduced. Children under eleven had two hours of schooling each day. Four factory inspectors were appointed to ensure the law was enforced.
1844	Children aged between eight and thirteen were only allowed to work six and a half hours a day. Children under the age of eighteen and women should work no more than twelve hours a day. All dangerous machinery had to be fenced off.
1847	Women and children under the age of eighteen should work a maximum of ten hours a day.
1867	The terms of the earlier Acts were applied to all workplaces in which more than five people were employed.

Even after these laws were passed, some factory owners continued to break them.

- Why do you think some factory owners did this?

- What parts of these laws would be the hardest to enforce?

- How does the government today protect children under sixteen at work?

- How does the government today protect adult workers?

TASKS...

A revolution is a complete change. It is often a sudden event leading to dramatic changes. Do you think the changes in industry were a 'revolution'? Give reasons for your answer.

Plenary

Imagine a local museum is creating an exhibition about working conditions for children in the nineteenth century. If you could include only one source from this entire section (pages 27–33) as an exhibit, which would it be? Why? Summarise your decision in no more than 50 words. Share your ideas with the rest of the class.

HOW DID THE RAILWAYS CHANGE BRITAIN?

Objectives

In this section you will find out:
- how and why railways developed
- how railways helped industry
- how railways improved people's leisure time.

To investigate these ideas you will:
- compare sources to make judgements about early railway engines
- classify the effects of the railways on a mind map.

Top speed, 100 mph.	Top speed, 125 mph.
London to Fishguard in 5 hours.	London to Fishguard in 4 hours 28 minutes.
Five carriages carrying up to 284 passengers; 42 first-class seats.	Five first-class carriages; one third-class carriage; one mail van; two dining carriages.
Driver and fireman on each engine; one guard at the back of the train and several attendants in dining carriages.	One driver; one train manager; two customer service hosts.
Buffet car with standing room only from London to Cardiff; trolley service on connecting train from Cardiff to Fishguard.	First-class dining with silver service waiters; full three-course meal available.
First-class return ticket, £157.	First-class return ticket, £56 to £197.

Starter

Look at the statements on this page. The facts and figures describe the train journey from London to Fishguard (which is in west Wales) in two different centuries. Then answer the questions that follow.

- *Which statements do you think describe the journey in 1909? Which describe the journey in 2002?*

- *Which journey do you think offers the most comfort and value for money?* **WS**

Facts and figures that describe the train journey from London to Fishguard in two different centuries.

The potential of railways

There had been some important developments in road and canal transport in the late eighteenth and early nineteenth centuries. These changes made travelling around the country easier. However, by far the greatest development came in the form of the railways which provided a faster and more comfortable solution to transport problems.

The statements you looked at in the Starter exercise on page 35 tell you something about the impact of railways. In this chapter you will find out more about this revolutionary form of transport.

Primitive railways with horses pulling wagons on wooden and later cast iron tracks had been used for many years in local industry. People such as Richard Trevithick had begun to experiment with steam engines in the early nineteenth century.

TASKS...

Working in pairs, imagine you are one of the judges at the Rainhill Trials. Look at each of the three main competitors on page 37. Then decide which engine you think should be awarded the £500 prize, and why.

Note: to be eligible for the prize, the engines must:
- weigh no more than six tons
- be able to pull carriages equal to three times the weight of the engine itself
- travel at speeds in excess of sixteen kilometres per hour.

Share your decision with the class. Then take a class vote to decide the winning engine. Once you find out the real result, compare this with the class vote winner. Did you agree with the judges at the time?

The Rainhill Trials

One of the first successful railways built was the Liverpool to Manchester railway, which opened in 1830. This opening followed the Rainhill Trials, which took place outside Liverpool in 1829 to decide the best type of steam locomotive to be used on the new railway. The railway company offered a prize of £500 for the winning design, and the competition itself attracted a crowd of 15,000 excited people. Ten locomotives were originally entered for the competition, but only five turned up. Each locomotive had to run twenty times up and down the track at Rainhill, which made the distance roughly equivalent to a return trip between Liverpool and Manchester.

The three main competitors

Engine 1: The Sans Pareil by Mr Hackworth of Darlington

Weight: 4 tons

Pulling power: 12 tons

Speed: unknown

Reliability: The boiler burst during the trial, so the engine was not able to complete its run; a compact design made the engine steady when travelling.

Engine 2: The Rocket by Mr Robert Stephenson of Newcastle

Weight: 4 tons

Pulling power: 17 tons

Speed: 22 kilometres an hour

Reliability: No breakdowns during the trial, so it was able to complete its run; a high chimney made the engine a little unsteady when travelling, which meant it swayed from side to side.

Engine 3: The Novelty by Mr Braithwaite and Mr Ericsson of London

Weight: 2 tons

Pulling power: 6 tons

Speed: up to 45 kilometres an hour

Reliability: Failed to complete the trials because the joints of the boiler gave way; however, the engine was light, compact and speedy.

After studying all the evidence, the three judges at the Rainhill Trials awarded the £500 first prize to the owners of the *Rocket*. The inventor of the *Rocket*, Robert Stephenson, won the contract to produce locomotives for the Liverpool and Manchester Railway and the railway line was opened in 1830.

How did the railways change industry and leisure time?

Following the success of the Liverpool to Manchester railway and Robert Stephenson's *Rocket*, railways became big business and thousands of miles of track were laid in the years that followed. Many navvies (navigators) and other workers were employed in the railway construction industry. In fact, in 1847 over 250,000 people were employed in the industry.

The construction of the railways also led to an increase in demand for iron and coal. Towns and cities all over the country had to build stations and clear land for platforms. When the railways were expanding, cities outside London became more attractive to businessmen who began to move their trades to cities such as Birmingham, Glasgow and Manchester.

The following statements explain how the railways changed people's work and leisure time.

1 Railways provided employment for thousands of men, particularly in the 1840s.

2 Suburbs were created on the edge of towns as workers could live there and go to work on the train.

3 Many canals were no longer used and went out of business.

4 Seaside resorts such as Blackpool and Brighton became very popular, because people could take day trips and holidays by train.

5 Railway transport reduced the cost of coal, which meant there was more demand for it so the coal industry grew.

6 Railways needed lots of iron and steel, so these industries grew.

7 New towns such as Crewe and Swindon developed because of the railways.

8 A national postage system (the Penny Post) was set up using the railways.

9 Farmers could make more money by using the railways to send fresh food to towns and cities.

10 Sports and entertainment such as football and music halls became more popular as people could travel to matches and concerts cheaply by train.

11 The iron and steel industries were able to grow because coal was cheaper and plentiful. Coal was needed to fuel these industries.

12 People in towns had a healthier diet, because fresh food was more readily available.

13 National newspapers became more widely read as they could be delivered around Britain on the same day.

14 Thousands of navvies suffered injuries or even died while building the railways.

15 Many homes were demolished in the big cities, particularly London, to build large railway stations.

16 Until a new law in 1846 the width of railway tracks varied, making travel between different areas difficult.

17 Trade and exports increased as goods could be transported much further afield.

TASKS...

1 The statements on pages 38–9 explain different effects of the railways on Britain.

  a) In pairs, sort these statements into two groups. The first group should show the economic effects of the railways (things to do with money and industry). The second group should show the social effects (things to do with the way people lived their lives).

  b) How else do you think you could you classify these statements?

2 Design a mind map using the outline suggested below to show the results of your thinking.

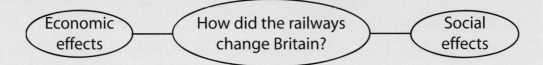

Economic effects ── How did the railways change Britain? ── Social effects

3 Look again at your mind map. What links can you see between the different effects? Draw arrows on your diagram to show these links. Over the top of each arrow you should explain why you think the points are linked.

4 Use your mind map to answer the question '*How did the railways change Britain?*' In your conclusion you should say which effect(s) you think were the most important. Make sure you clearly explain your choice.

Plenary

Read out your concluding paragraph (Task 4) to the rest of the class. Alternatively, get into groups of four and read out your concluding paragraphs to each other.

How far do you agree on what the most important effects of the railways were? Discuss this in groups.

WORKING-CLASS REACTIONS: DID EVERYONE AGREE WITH THE CHANGES IN AGRICULTURE AND INDUSTRY?

3

WHO WERE NED LUDD AND CAPTAIN SWING?

Objectives

In this section you will find out:

- who the Luddites and Swing Rioters were and the tactics they used
- why their protests took place and how successful they were
- the importance of their protests.

To investigate these ideas you will:

- assess a range of sources
- use information to produce a game of historical bingo.

Starter

Look at the two letters shown in Sources A and B.

SOURCE A

Sir,

Information has just been given in that you are an owner of those detestable shearing frames, and I was asked by my men to write to you and warn you to pull them down.

If they are not taken down by the end of next week, I will send one of my lieutenants with at least 300 men to destroy them. If we come, we will increase your misfortune by burning your buildings to ashes. If you fire upon any of my men, they have orders to murder you and burn all your housing.

Inform your neighbours that the same fate awaits them if their shearing frames are not speedily taken down, as I understand there are several in your neighbourhood.

A letter to Frederick Smith, a mill owner, from Ned Ludd, 1812.

SOURCE B

This is to inform you that if you don't pull down your machines and raise the wages of married men to two and six pence a day and single men to two shillings, we will burn down your barns and you in them. This is the last notice.

A letter from Captain Swing.

💡 *What do you think these letters are complaining about?*

💡 *What do you think the writers are threatening to do?*

💡 *Why do you think they feel they need to take such drastic action?*

Sometimes people resorted to violence to try to prevent changes taking place. In this section you will learn about two examples of this type of reaction.

SOURCE C

A cartoon of Ned Ludd dressed as a woman, c. 1810.

Who were the Luddites and the Swing Rioters?

The Luddites

Luddites were mainly industrial workers from Nottinghamshire, Leicestershire, Derbyshire, Yorkshire, Lancashire and Cheshire. Between 1811 and 1816, these workers destroyed machinery that they felt was threatening their way of life.

The leader of the Luddites was called Ned Ludd, but he was also known as Captain Ludd or King Ludd. One story suggests that Ned Ludd was an apprentice who destroyed his employers' equipment as revenge for a beating. He was supposed to live secretly in Sherwood Forest. He was almost certainly a fictional character.

💡 What impression of Ned Ludd do you think Source C gives?

The Swing Rioters

Swing Rioters were agricultural workers, mainly from the south of England, who rioted in the autumn of 1830 in order to improve their standard of living. The first riots broke out in Kent but quickly spread to 22 other counties – including Sussex, Berkshire, Oxfordshire, Suffolk, Norfolk, Cambridgeshire, Gloucestershire and Buckinghamshire.

The leader of the Swing Rioters was known as Captain Swing. It is likely that he, too, was a fictional character. One historian suggests that the name 'Swing' was inspired by the **flail** used in threshing, because it swings when it is being used.

Why did the Luddites protest?

A modern photograph of a steam-powered loom. This machine put people out of work.

The impact of new machinery

The Luddites protested about changes in industry – particularly the introduction of new machinery into the textile industry. This machinery did not require skilled operators and could only be used in factories. Skilled craftsmen, who had previously earned high wages and worked at their own pace, began to lose their income and faced ruin. Many believed they could force the factory owners not to use the new machines.

Hard times

Workers were also vulnerable to big variations in the price of bread, especially when harvests were bad. Crop failures between 1809 and 1812 resulted in increased prices: by 1812 bread prices were double what they had been in 1802. This coincided with a depression in industry from 1811 that led to wages being lowered. In 1812 hand-loom weavers were earning less than half what they had been earning in 1802. There was also widespread unemployment.

Skilled craftsmen did not have the vote, so they could not put pressure on the government to help them.

💡 Why do you think some industrial workers felt so desperate in 1812?

💡 Why do you think they felt that violence was their only option?

Why did the Swing Rioters protest?

At the beginning of the nineteenth century, farming was in a depression.

● After 1815 there were too many agricultural labourers partly because of the end of the Napoleonic Wars (see page 18) and partly because of the effects of enclosure (see pages 14–18). It became much harder to find work. This resulted in lower wages for the labourers.

● Between 1828 and 1830, harvests were poor. This resulted in a rise in unemployment in rural areas and increased bread prices. Poverty and hardship became more widespread.

The impact of new machinery

One of the main jobs done by farm workers in the winter months was threshing. In the late 1820s and early 1830s many farmers in the south of England began introducing steam-powered threshing machines. Many farm labourers were faced with the prospect of unemployment and having to depend on poor relief at the hardest time of the year. The new threshing machines became a source of hatred.

Agricultural labourers did not have the vote so they could not put pressure on the government to help them. To add to this period of hardship, the amount given in poor relief between 1815 and 1830 fell by about a quarter and it became harder to get help.

💡 Why do you think agricultural workers felt so desperate by 1830?

💡 Why do you think that agricultural workers thought violence was their only option?

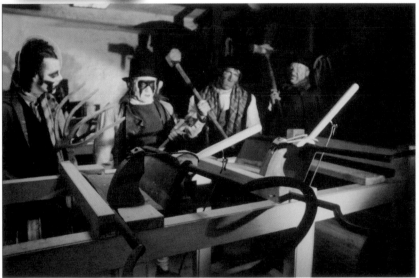

Luddites smashing machinery. The photograph shows actors from a television documentary, *The Luddites*, shown in 1988.

What tactics did the Luddites use?

The main Luddite tactic involved breaking into factories at night. They often did this in disguise. They would vandalise machines, burn down factories and attack factory owners. Between March 1811 and February 1812, Luddites in Nottinghamshire destroyed about 1000 machines.

One of the most famous attacks by the Luddites took place in Yorkshire. Rawfolds Mill, which was owned by William Cartwright and located in Brighouse, was the target. On 11 April 1812 about 150 Luddites led by George Mellor attacked the mill. The mill was defended by soldiers. The Luddites failed to gain entry and two of them were killed in the process. A week later, an attempt was made to murder Cartwright. On 28 April another mill owner from the area, William Horsfall, was murdered.

What tactics did the Swing Rioters use?

The Swing Rioters used a range of methods, including destroying machinery – more than 350 threshing machines were destroyed by the Swing Rioters in the south of England. Additionally, they used arson and burned down many **hayricks**. They sent threatening letters to farmers, some of whom were also attacked. They often damaged farm buildings.

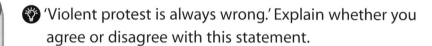 'Violent protest is always wrong.' Explain whether you agree or disagree with this statement.

How did the government react?

The government dealt harshly with the Luddites, because it was worried that their activities would cause a revolution in Britain.

In February 1812 the government passed the Frame Breaking Act. People who were found guilty of breaking weaving machines could be sentenced to death. The government ordered nearly 12,000 troops into the areas where Luddite protest was common to help defend factories and keep order. Luddites were severely punished. For example, fourteen were hanged for their attack on Rawfolds Mill and three were executed for the murder of William Horsfall. Fourteen others were **transported** as convicts.

The government took firm action against the Swing Rioters and some 2000 people in 34 counties were put on trial. Those found guilty were harshly punished: 19 were hanged, 644 were imprisoned, and 481 men were transported.

Do you think the Luddites or Swing Rioters could ever win their fight? Explain your opinion.

Did the protests achieve anything?

The Luddites

The Luddites didn't really achieve anything. After 1820 nothing more was heard of them. Not only that, the machines stayed.

The Swing Rioters

In some areas wages did rise and some farmers got rid of their threshing machines. However, farm labourers continued to be very badly paid and the problem of poverty remained.

💡 Today, some people criticise others by saying 'You're a Luddite'. What do you think they mean by saying that?

💡 A revolutionary is someone who wants to bring about a complete or dramatic change. Were the Luddites or the Swing Rioters revolutionaries? Explain your answer.

TASKS...

In small groups, produce a game of historical bingo to test your understanding of this section.

1   To begin with, create twelve explanation cards and twelve answer cards that cover the information you have studied. An example of an explanation card might be: 'The leader of this organisation was supposed to live secretly in Sherwood Forest.' The corresponding answer card would be: 'The Luddites'.

2   To play your game, swap your cards with another group.
   a) One member of the group acts as the host, with the others as contestants. The host will give the contestants a bingo card and the twelve answer cards to choose from. The contestants should not see the explanation cards.
   b) The contestants write nine answers onto their card. The host then randomly draws explanations from a bag and puts them on the desk. Contestants cross off the answer the explanation refers to.
   c) When a contestant gets a consecutive horizontal line, he or she reads back the terms and definitions correctly. If a mistake is made, continue with the game.
   d) Repeat the process for a consecutive vertical line and full house.

3   Evaluate the bingo game. What improvements do you think you could make? Try to suggest at least three ways.

Plenary

Carefully study Source F.

A cartoon of 1830 about the Swing Riots.

What evidence is there that the supporters of Captain Swing used violence?

Who do you think is being threatened in the cartoon?

Look at the two characters on the right. What do you think is the difference in their attitude towards the Swing Riots?

Which point of view do you think the cartoonist agreed with? Explain your answer carefully.

WHAT WAS CHARTISM AND HOW IMPORTANT WERE THE CHARTISTS?

Objectives

In this section you will find out:
- the causes of Chartism
- the tactics used by the Chartists and how successful the Chartists were.

To investigate these ideas you will:
- create a diagram to show the causes of Chartism
- interpret a range of sources to assess whether Chartism succeeded or failed.

Starter

Read Source A.

SOURCE A

> 1 A VOTE for every man twenty-one years of age, of sound mind, and not undergoing punishment for crime.
>
> 2 SECRET BALLOT – to protect the elector in the exercise of his vote.
>
> 3 NO PROPERTY QUALIFICATION for Members of Parliament – thus enabling the **constituencies** to return the man of his choice, be he rich or poor.
>
> 4 PAYMENT OF MEMBERS, thus enabling an honest tradesman, working man, or other person to serve a constituency, when taken from his business to attend to the interests of the country.
>
> 5 EQUAL CONSTITUENCIES, securing the same amount of representation for the same number of electors, instead of allowing small constituencies to swamp the vote of large ones.
>
> 6 ANNUAL PARLIAMENTS, thus presenting the most effectual check to bribery and intimidation, since though a constituency might be bought once in seven years (even with the **ballot**), no purse could buy a constituency (under a system of universal **suffrage**) in each ensuring twelve month; and since members, when elected for a year only, would not be able to defy and betray their constituents as now.

The six points of the People's Charter. This text is taken from a handbill handed out in the streets of Britain in 1838.

Key words

Constituency A town, part of a town or a rural area that elects a Member of Parliament.

Ballot Vote.

Suffrage The right to vote.

WORKING-CLASS REACTIONS.

💡 *What did the Chartists think was wrong with the political system?*

💡 *What do you think the Chartists wanted?*

💡 *Which of their demands are law today?*

💡 *Can you think of any reasons why one of the demands is not law today?*
Explain your answer.

💡 *Point one of the charter only mentions men. Should it be called the People's Charter?*

How did the Chartists form?

In 1836 a group of working men set up the London Working Men's Association (LWMA). The association's secretary was William Lovett. Other leaders included Francis Place and Henry Hetherington. Chartism, as the movement became known after the charter it drew up in 1838, was not only based in London. It also attracted support from across Britain. One group, led by Feargus O'Connor, set up a newspaper, *The Northern Star*. In 1838, there were Chartist groups all over the country.

What were the causes of Chartism?

Outbreaks of diseases such as cholera and smallpox. These led to many ordinary people wanting their living conditions improved.

Hatred of the 1834 Poor Law Amendment Act. Poverty was treated almost as a crime. Workhouses were hated because of their brutal conditions.

Dislike of the new conditions in the nineteenth-century factories (for example discipline and low wages).

Disappointment over the 1833 Factory Act – it did nothing for adults and only applied to the textile industry.

The causes of Chartism

Trade unions had limited power to bargain with employers. The government usually backed employers in disputes.

Disappointment over the 1832 Reform Act. The working classes had taken part in demonstrations for reform, but did not get the vote in 1832 (see page 67).

Unemployment (the spread of factories and machinery put some people out of work).

High taxation.

High food prices when harvests were bad.

Chartists believed that if working people could have the vote, they could do something about their other complaints.

TASKS...

1 Look at the causes of Chartism shown on the spider diagram on page 50. Using a diagram like the one below, sort these causes into political, economic and social complaints. Use the overlap areas for causes that fit into more than one category. **WS**

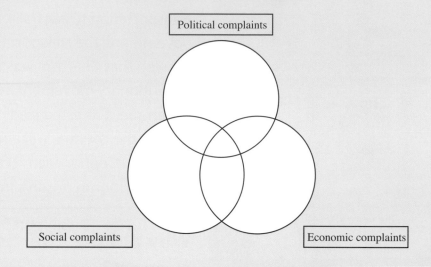

Political complaints

Social complaints

Economic complaints

What tactics did the Chartists use?

In 1838 the LWMA drew up a list of demands that became known as the People's Charter. It soon became clear that the leaders of the Chartist movement had different ideas about what should happen next. William Lovett and his supporters believed that only persuasion or 'moral force' should be used to get Parliament to accept the Charter. However, Feargus O'Connor and his supporters believed that violence or 'physical force' should be used.

Key words

Petition A request, often signed by many people.

In May 1839 the Chartists presented a **petition** to Parliament supporting the Charter. More than 1.25 million people signed it. In July 1839 it was rejected in Parliament by 235 votes to 46. Following this rejection, there were outbreaks of violence.

The most serious outbreak took place at Newport, South Wales. On 4 November, after the arrest of a popular Chartist leader, Henry Vincent, local Chartists marched on the hotel where they believed Vincent was being held. They were met by a force of special constables and soldiers. It isn't clear what happened next, but shots were fired and many Chartists were killed.

Over the next few days some 90 Chartists were arrested. Eight Chartists were sentenced to death, although this sentence was later reduced to transportation to Australia. For the government, the Newport Rising showed that Chartism was a revolutionary movement, so the government arrested leading Chartists around the country. William Lovett and Feargus O'Connor each received eighteen-month prison sentences.

The Chartist riot at Newport in 1839.

Why did the Chartists lose support?

After 1839 the Chartists lost support. A slump in trade in 1842 led to unemployment, poverty and hunger in many industrial areas. Feargus O'Connor set up the National Charter Association to organise a second petition. This time, more than three million people signed it.

Thousands of people marched to Parliament to hand this petition over. It needed 50 men to hand it in to the House of Commons. In May, Parliament once again rejected the Charter by 287 votes to 49. In the summer of 1842, workers from the midlands and the north who supported Chartism decided to go on strike. Some of these strikers stopped all work being done in their factories by removing boiler plugs from the steam engines. As a result, these strikes became known as the 'Plug Plot'.

The strikes soon ended and protesters returned to work. About 1500 people were arrested for their part in these strikes. Some seventy were found guilty and sentenced to between seven and twenty-one years' transportation. After 1842 support for Chartism declined as economic conditions improved.

What revived Chartism again?

In 1847 support for Chartism began to revive. Unemployment was high, poor harvests had led to a rise in food prices, and there were outbreaks of cholera and smallpox. Feargus O'Connor began to organise a third petition. This time, the Chartists claimed they had collected six million signatures.

O'Connor planned a mass meeting of half a million people on Kennington Common in London on 10 April 1848. This meeting would be followed by a march to Parliament to hand over the petition. The government expected trouble and over 80,000 special constables were put on standby.

An engraving of 1848 showing the Chartist rally at Kennington Common.

In the end, O'Connor's plans were dashed. Only about 20,000 Chartists turned up, which meant there were more constables than protesters! And only O'Connor was allowed to take the petition to Parliament. The rest of the crowd was forced to disperse.

When the petition was inspected it had only 1.9 million real signatures. Among the rest were signatures such as Victoria Rex, Prince of Wales, Sir Robert Peel and Duke of Wellington, plus false names such as Pugnose, Longnose, Flatnose, Snooks, Fobb and No Cheese. Parliament rejected the Charter by 222 votes to 17. After this fiasco, Chartism as a mass movement came to an end.

TASKS...

1 Why do you think so many people signed the charters in 1839, 1842 and 1848?

2 Do you think the Newport Rising in 1839 and the Plug Plot in 1842 helped or harmed Chartism? Explain your answer carefully.

3 Why was 1848 a disaster for Chartism?

Was Chartism a complete failure?

1 *Parliament refused to support the Charter.*

2 *Factory Acts improved working conditions for many people.*

3 *The middle class opposed the movement.*

4 *Chartists were divided among themselves.*

5 *Five of the six points of the Charter eventually became law.*
- *In 1858, the property qualification for MPs was abolished.*
- *The vote was extended in 1867, 1884, 1918, 1928 and 1969.*
- *The secret ballot was introduced in 1872.*
- *In 1885 electoral districts were made roughly equal.*
- *In 1911 MPs finally got a wage.*

6 *Chartist demands were too extreme for the time.*

7 *Chartism was made to look foolish because of the 1848 petition.*

8 *The Public Health Acts in the second half of the nineteenth century improved living conditions and made towns healthier.*

9 *Chartism only flourished when times were hard. When economic conditions improved, Chartism lost its appeal.*

💡 Why do you think Chartism did less well at times of economic prosperity?

TASKS...

1 Take a look at the statements 1 to 9 above. Sort them into two lists:

   a) reasons why Chartism failed

   b) changes that Chartism helped to achieve in the long run.

TASKS...

2 Look at the two statements below.

> *Chartism was doomed to fail from the beginning because it lacked effective leadership.*

> *Chartism was a complete failure. Working men had not achieved the vote by 1848.*

Explain how a historian sympathetic towards Chartism would answer these criticisms. Use the statements you sorted in task 1 to help you.

3 Were the Chartists revolutionary? Explain your opinion carefully.

EXTENSION TASK...

Other examples of how the working class reacted to the changes caused by the revolutions include:
- the Rebecca riots
- the formation of trade unions.

Find out how sucessful these reactions were. Were they revolutionary?

Plenary

Look at Source D.

What reasons do you think Source D suggests for the rejection of the Charter?

Can you think of any other reasons why the government refused to accept Chartist ideas? Explain your answer.

A contemporary cartoon commenting on the debate in the House of Commons in 1848 over the Charter.

WHICH PROTEST ACHIEVED THE MOST?
TASKS...

1   You are now going to conclude your investigation by producing a piece of extended writing that will explain which of the protest movements you think achieved the most and why. To help you reach that decision, and to help you to explain your reasoning, copy and complete the chart below for each protest movement you have learned about in this chapter. Try to use your own words wherever possible, as this shows greater understanding, and use key points only. **WS**

Protest movement	Aims	Tactics used	How the government reacted	What the movement achieved
The Luddites				
The Swing Rioters				
The Chartists				

2   Now use your chart to answer the question: *'Which protest movement achieved the most, and why was it more successful than the others?'*

Plenary

In small groups discuss the different methods people use to protest. Classify these into violent and non-violent methods.

What measures are there in today's society to make violent protest less likely?

Share your ideas with the rest of the class.

WHAT POLITICAL HURDLES DID PEOPLE HAVE TO OVERCOME TO GAIN THE VOTE?

WHAT WAS WRONG WITH THE ELECTORAL SYSTEM IN THE 1800s?

Objectives

In this section you will find out:
- the problems with the electoral system in the 1800s.

To investigate this idea you will:
- study the reactions of people towards the electoral system in the 1800s
- complete a living graph and diary planner to show what political hurdles people had to overcome to gain the vote.

Starter

Look at Source A below. Then read the statements of the five characters on page 58 and answer the questions that follow.

SOURCE A

A political cartoon published in 1832.

The Reformers' Attack on the Old Rotten Tree; or, the Foul Nests of the Cormorants in Danger.

Key words

Democratic right The right to elect people as representatives in government.

Borough A town that elected two MPs. The rules of who could vote in boroughs varied from area to area.

I am 35 years old and I live in south-west England. I own lots of land and several houses. I am a very important lady in my area. Everyone knows me and asks for my advice. Despite being very well educated, I have no political rights and am unable to vote. This is because I am a woman.

A rich lady.

I am a landowner from Cornwall. I am very rich and rent out my land to local farmers. I have represented the people of Cornwall as an MP for many years because I can influence the way they vote by bribing and threatening them.

A landowner from Cornwall.

Key words

County Rural areas where only property owners could vote.

Rotten borough Boroughs with small numbers of voters who could be bribed. Votes could be sold to the highest bidder.

*I am a rich industrialist based in Manchester. I own several factories. But I am unable to vote because those who live in the north of the country have no **democratic rights** and are not represented in Parliament.*

A rich factory owner.

*I work very hard farming the land to support my young family. I have no democratic rights because I cannot vote. They say that it's because I don't own my own house and that I live in a **borough**, not a **county**. Why should it matter where I live?*

A working-class man.

*I live in a tiny old village with just ten other houses. I am allowed to vote and our tiny village elects two MPs to Parliament. Sometimes we make money by selling our votes to men who really want to become MPs. Our area is sometimes called a **rotten borough** and some people believe that we should not be allowed to elect two MPs.*

A property owner from a small village.

Hurdles to voting in the 1800s

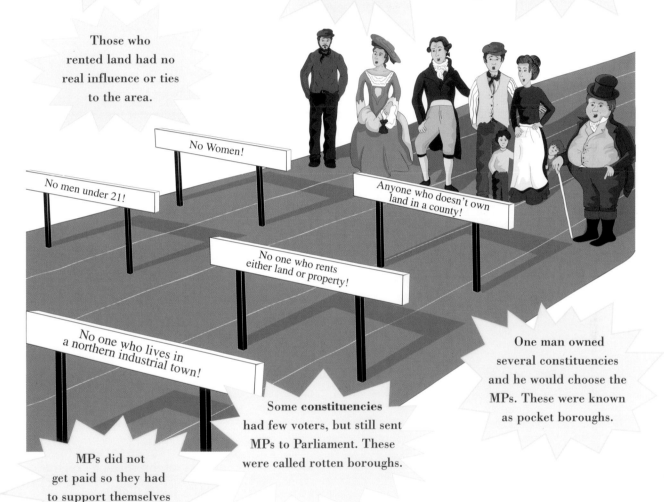

Northern industrial towns were newly formed and had no influence because they did not send MPs to Parliament in London.

Women were seen as unstable and incapable of dealing with the pressure of voting.

Elections could last several weeks. It was easy to bribe and threaten voters, as elections would take place in public.

Those who rented land had no real influence or ties to the area.

No Women!

No men under 21!

Anyone who doesn't own land in a county!

No one who rents either land or property!

No one who lives in a northern industrial town!

One man owned several constituencies and he would choose the MPs. These were known as pocket boroughs.

Some **constituencies** had few voters, but still sent MPs to Parliament. These were called rotten boroughs.

MPs did not get paid so they had to support themselves while in Parliament.

Areas were divided into constituencies, called counties and boroughs; these varied in size and in the number of inhabitants. Whether you could vote depended on where you lived.

Key words

Constituency An area represented in Parliament by an elected MP.

Key words

Electoral system The way in which people vote for the government.

💡 What criticisms do you think some people had of the **electoral system** in the 1800s?

💡 Why do you think some people favoured the electoral system in the 1800s?

💡 How do you think the five characters might react to the political illustration in Source A on page 57?

💡 Which side of the tree do you think the five characters would be standing on in Source A? Explain your decision.

TASKS...

1 Look at the illustrations on pages 58–9 then answer the following questions.

  a) What problems do you think people faced if they wanted to become an MP?

  b) Who do you think had to overcome the most hurdles in 1800 in order to get the vote?

2 Throughout this chapter you will use a living graph and a diary planner to follow how electoral reforms affected the five characters you met on page 58.

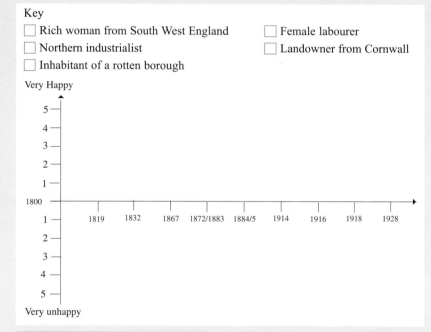

Key
☐ Rich woman from South West England   ☐ Female labourer
☐ Northern industrialist   ☐ Landowner from Cornwall
☐ Inhabitant of a rotten borough

Very Happy

5
4
3
2
1
1800
1   1819   1832   1867   1872/1883   1884/5   1914   1916   1918   1928
2
3
4
5

Very unhappy

A living graph to show the impact of electoral reforms on individuals.

a) Copy the living graph into your book and plot the position of each character in 1800 onto the graph. **WS**

b) Fill in a diary entry for each character in order to: **WS**

- explain how the character would have felt about the electoral system in 1800
- justify your placement of the character on the living graph.

Plenary

Write down five reasons why you think the electoral system in 1800 was unfair. Compare your list with a partner. How are your reasons similar? How are they different?

WHY DID SOME PEOPLE BELIEVE THAT ELECTORAL REFORM WAS NEEDED?

Objectives

In this section you will find out:
- which people believed electoral reform was needed
- why they believed that electoral reform was needed.

To investigate these ideas you will:
- select and categorise evidence
- use this evidence to write a speech.

Starter

Take a look at the three characters below, then answer the questions. You will find information about these characters on page 58.

💡 *Which of these characters do you think is the odd one out?*

💡 *Which character do you think was most unfairly treated by the electoral system in the 1800s? Why?*

The electoral system in the early 1800s

More and more people were becoming dissatisfied with the electoral system in the early 1800s. After 1815 things began to get worse for many people. Soldiers returning to Britain from the Napoleonic Wars found there were not enough jobs for all of them, so unemployment increased. Bread prices were also high and people experienced great hardship. Many people believed that gaining the vote would help to solve their problems, though not everyone wanted change in the electoral system.

Some opinions about the electoral system in the early 1800s

1 There is no need to change anything – our system has worked well for years. It is the best in the world; everyone benefits from it.

2 Only the wealthy should vote. They have the most influence because they own the land. You should only be allowed a say in the running of the country if you own some land.

3 Those people elected as MPs are out of touch with the needs of working-class people. The government only looks after the rich and that's unfair.

4 Many people don't understand the voting process. It will be a disaster if **the masses** are allowed to vote. The economy will suffer if people who don't understand it influence laws. There will be a revolution if unskilled workers and women are allowed to vote.

5 Industrialists make the money, so we need industrialists to become MPs. Industrialists and entrepreneurs should be represented so that Britain's industrial future can be properly planned.

6 The middle classes should vote. They will make our country more successful.

7 Changes are needed so that more people can be properly represented in Parliament. The poor are not represented and wages have been cut. There is a need to pass new reforms that can improve their lives.

8 It is unfair that some people can buy parliamentary seats. Bribery and corruption is not the way forward. Why should only the rich become MPs?

9 How can a borough with six houses have two MPs but a newly formed town with thousands have no MP?

10 A woman is not inferior to a man; women work hard to provide for their families.

11 Why should it matter whether people live in boroughs or counties?

Key words

The masses The majority of the people.

TASKS...

1 Look at the statements on page 62, which give arguments for and arguments against electoral reform in the 1800's.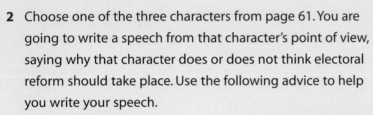

   a) Copy the Venn diagram (right) into your books twice. Above one of the diagrams write the title: '*Arguments for electoral reform*'. Above the second diagram write the title: '*Arguments against electoral refom*'.

   b) Categorise the different arguments for and against electoral reform by writing the statement numbers in the correct places on the two diagrams. Some of the arguments may reflect two factors or even all three factors – you will need to write these numbers in the correct overlap on the Venn diagram.

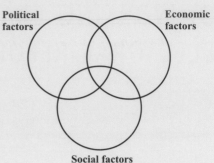

2 Choose one of the three characters from page 61. You are going to write a speech from that character's point of view, saying why that character does or does not think electoral reform should take place. Use the following advice to help you write your speech.

- Write an introduction that sets out your character's opinion of the electoral system in the nineteenth century.
- List the arguments that support your character's point of view.
- List the arguments that oppose your character's point of view.
- Summarise your speech by reinforcing your character's opinion of the electoral system in the nineteenth century.

Key words

Economic factors Reasons connected with money.

Political factors Reasons connected with politics and government.

Social factors Reasons connected with people and society.

Plenary

In pairs or groups, discuss the following questions.

💡 Which of the three characters from page 61 do you think the government would take most notice of? Why?

💡 Which character do you think the government would take least notice of? Why?

HOW EFFECTIVE WERE THE CAMPAIGNS OF WORKING-CLASS MOVEMENTS FOR ELECTORAL REFORM?

Objectives

In this section you will find out:
- what methods were used by the working-class to campaign for electoral reform before and after 1832
- how successful these methods were in bringing about electoral reform.

To investigate these ideas you will:
- study evidence that shows the impact of electoral reform
- continue work on the living graph and diary planner that you began on page 60.

Starter

In pairs, look at Source A.

The Massacre of Peterloo by the political cartoonist, George Cruickshank, published in 1819.

Imagine you are somewhere in the picture in Source A, but do not tell your partner where. Using the labels and the key words on the cartoon, describe to your partner what 'you' can see, hear and smell, and what your feelings about the actual event are. Once your partner has found 'you' on the picture, swap roles.

 What three questions would you like to ask in order to find out more about the background to Source A?

What actually happened at the Peterloo Massacre?

Key words

Orator Public speaker.

A radical Someone who wants major changes in society.

Cavalry Soldiers on horseback.

Sabre A curved sword.

On 16 August 1819 almost 60,000 middle and working-class men, women and children gathered at St Peter's Field in Manchester to hear Henry '**Orator**' Hunt, Mary Fildes and other **radical** political reformers talk about the problems that they and many other people were experiencing.

The local magistrates who were responsible for the safety of the crowds were worried that there might be a riot. They were not used to such large meetings taking place and so they called out the local yeomanry – a poorly organised, part-time **cavalry** force – along with the regular cavalry to sort out any problems. At approximately 1.40 pm, when Henry Hunt began to address the crowds, the yeomanry pushed their way through to arrest him. The cavalry charged into the crowd to help them. This caused mass panic among both horses and people. The result was a massive stampede.

Many of the regular cavalry attacked the public with their **sabres** while trying to reach and arrest Henry Hunt and the other speakers. Eleven people were killed and about 400 were injured.

… prompt, decisive and efficient measures for the preservation of the public peace.

The government's description of the magistrates' actions at Peterloo in 1819.

Over the field were strewn caps, bonnets, hats, shawls and shoes and other parts of male and female dress, trampled, torn and bloody. The yeomanry had dismounted – some were easing their horses … others were wiping their sabres.

A description by a radical politician of St Peter's Field after the Peterloo Massacre .

 How do Sources B and C differ in their interpretations of events on 16 August 1819?

💡 *Why do you think the writers have such different views about what happened at St Peters Field?*

💡 *How useful are these interpretations in finding out about events on the 16 August 1819? Explain your answer clearly.*

TASKS...

WS Imagine you are a newspaper journalist. It is your job to write a report of the event at St Peter's Field in Manchester, which would support either Source B or Source C on page 65. You must use bias and emotional language to back up your view. You may want to use the words below to help you with your report.

Examples of words that could be used to support the magistrates	*Examples of words that could be used to support the reformers*
brave	*cowardly*
riot	*unprofessional*
attacked	*brutal*
unorganised	*hacking*
provoked	*blood-thirsty*
	massacre

What effects did the Peterloo Massacre have on electoral reform?

The government was shocked at the events at Peterloo and decided not to change the electoral system while there was so much unrest throughout Britain. In December 1819 the government passed the Six Acts, to try to control this unrest.

The Six Acts, 1819

- *Public meetings were restricted.*
- *Newspapers and leaflets that might provoke public unrest could not be printed.*
- *Magistrates were given greater powers to control and imprison people.*
- *The government refused to consider political reform.*

TASKS...

1 Look back to page 60 and to the living graph and diary planner that you started. Remind yourselves of the five characters by re-reading page 58.

   a) Use your living graph to plot the position of each character in 1819 after the Six Acts were introduced.

   b) For each character, explain in your diary planner where you have placed them on the graph and why.

2 What impact did the working class have on electoral reform before 1832? Explain your answer.

How successful were campaigns for electoral reform after 1832?

The Six Acts of 1819 stopped working-class people from campaigning effectively for electoral reform. However, during this time the government began to take notice of the complaints of working-class people and started to make some changes. Between 1832 and 1884 the government passed a series of electoral reforms.

The Great Reform Act of 1832

Constituencies were rearranged to make them fairer and more equal:

- 56 rotten boroughs were abolished
- 30 boroughs with a population of fewer than 4000 could now elect only one MP
- voters in industrial towns were now able to elect a total of 142 MPs.

In addition, more people were given the vote: the number of voters rose by 200,000. After 1832 approximately one in five men could vote in parliamentary elections.

However, the Great Reform Act of 1832 did not give the vote to everybody:

- working-class men still could not vote
- woman could not vote
- being given the vote still depended on where you lived
- bribery and corruption continued in the electoral system.

The Great Reform Act of 1867

- All male householders in boroughs could vote.
- 45 extra MPs were elected from industrial towns.
- 45 boroughs with a population under 10,000 elected one MP only.
- The number of voters increased by one million.

However, women and men in some counties still did not have the vote.

The Secret Ballot Act of 1872 and the Corrupt Practices Act of 1883

- Landlords and employers could no longer bribe or threaten workers and tenants to vote for a particular political party.
- People running for election had to explain all their expenses.
- Bribery and corruption were to be punished.

The Reform Act of 1884–5

- Boroughs where less than 15,000 people lived were abolished, that is not allowed to elect an MP.
- In most areas, men could now vote.
- All male householders could vote.
- The number of voters increased by two million.
- There was to be one MP for each constituency throughout the country.

Remaining problems

Those men who had not been living in an area for long enough or did not own a house could still not vote. The right to vote was linked to ownership of property, so some people had two votes because they owned property in two different areas. There were also still problems with the size of the constituencies.

TASKS...

1. Look at your living graph and diary planner, which you last updated on page 66. Remind yourselves of the five characters by re-reading page 58.
   a) Now use your living graph to plot the impact on each character of the Acts passed between 1832 and 1885.
   b) For each character, explain in your diary planner where you have placed them on the graph and why.

2. Which Act do you think had the greatest impact on electoral reform? Explain your answer.

Plenary

Choose one of the five characters outlined on page 58. How do you think he or she would have viewed these Acts? Explain your answer. Share your answers with a partner.

HOW EFFECTIVELY DID WOMEN'S SUFFRAGE GROUPS CAMPAIGN FOR ELECTORAL REFORM?

Objectives

In this section you will find out:
- the differences between Suffragists and Suffragettes
- the degree of opposition to women campaigning for the right to vote
- why women's campaigns for the right to vote came to an end.

To investigate these ideas you will:
- use information to understand more about the Suffragists and Suffragettes
- use source material to discover who opposed votes for women
- complete the living graph and diary planner that you have been working on throughout this chapter.

Starter

Imagine it is the early-twentieth century. You want to join an organisation that campaigns for women's suffrage, but you are undecided which group to join. Copy and complete the questionnaire on the right, which will help you to decide.

1 **You feel strongly about an issue and want others to listen to your thoughts. What do you do?**
a) Try to persuade others to listen to your point of view. ☐
b) Gain maximum publicity for your cause by making sure that everything you do is written about in the press. ☐

2 **You want those who live far away to know about your beliefs. How will you do this?**
a) Distribute leaflets and posters, and hold public meetings with guest speakers. ☐
b) Grab people's attention and make the newspaper headlines by smashing windows and chaining yourself to railings. ☐

3 **You want MPs to listen to your cause. How will you do this?**
a) Talk to MPs and send petitions so they know you are serious. ☐
b) Harass MPs, enter the House of Commons and disrupt public and private meetings so that they are forced to act on your behalf. ☐

4 **Someone fighting for your cause dies. How do you react?**
a) You don't make a big deal of it – the person's irrational and unpredictable behaviour may actually do your cause more harm than good. ☐
b) You treat this person as a martyr, organising a huge public funeral procession to highlight your cause. ☐

5 **MPs have broken a promise to you and change their mind on a law they were meant to pass. What do you do?**
a) Carry on your peaceful protests – people are taking you seriously and increasing numbers are following your cause. ☐
b) Use violent methods, and take them one step further by burning down a church and causing more chaos. ☐

Key words

Suffragist A member of the National Union of Women's Suffrage Societies (NUWSS).

Suffragette A member of the Women's Social and Political Union (WSPU), an organisation that sometimes used violence to further its aims.

Spinster An unmarried woman. The term was used usually to refer to women past the 'marrying age'.

Militant Aggressive.

*Now count up how many As and Bs you have scored. If you have chosen more As than Bs, you would probably join the **Suffragist** movement. If you have chosen more Bs than As, you would probably join the **Suffragette** movement. Read on to find out why …*

What was the difference between the Suffragists and the Suffragettes?

Millicent Fawcett, 1897 NUWSS (National Union of Women's Suffrage societies)

Emeline Pankhurst, 1903 WSPU (Women's Social and Political Union)

1867: middle-class and working class women belonged to the organisation.
1897: there were more than 500 local branches. Many liberal MPs supported the suffragists.
1910: 21, 571 members.

1910: 11 regional offices.
Often associated with wealthy middle-class **spinsters**.

The methods used were usually peaceful.

The methods used were often **militant**.

Petitions would be presented to MPs in Parliament, leaflets and letters were distributed, and MPs were put under constant pressure.

Political meetings were disrupted, MPs were harassed and threatened with violence. Suffragettes threw stones at windows, burned down buildings, smashed paintings.

They participated in public debates.

Organised speeches were held across the country.

We will get the vote.

We will get the vote.

Marches were well disciplined.

Suffragettes were often arrested.

The Suffragette is the militant lady who attempts by forcible means to interview Cabinet Ministers and Members of Parliament, and for whose safety large bodies of police are called out. They prefer a short rest in one of His Majesty's 'homes of seclusion' to the quiet domesticity of their own fireside, but as a rule they only try the experiment once.

   The Suffragist is a much quieter lady. She does not believe in the tactics of her sister, the warlike Suffragette, but is content to urge her claims for a vote simply by her own persuasive speaking.

From the *South London Press*, March 1908.

SOURCE B

What do you think is meant in Source A when the article refers to His Majesty's 'homes of seclusion'?

Suffragettes campaigning in London against the Liberal Party during the election of 1910.

SOURCE C

SOURCE D

Violent protests	5
Arson	11
Explosions	1
Window breaking	1
Telephone wire cutting	2
Use of chemicals	3
Meetings	89

An account of Suffragette activities in 1913, from the magazine *The Suffragette*

A suffragette chained to railings near Downing Street in 1910.

TASKS...

1 Look at the information on page 70 and Sources A to D on page 71.

    a) What were the differences between the Suffragists and Suffragettes?

    b) What were the strengths of each group?

    c) What were the weaknesses of each group?

    d) Do you think it would have been possible for the Suffragists and the Suffragettes to reach a compromise? Give reasons for your answer.

2 Imagine that a friend cannot decide whether to join the Suffragists or the Suffragettes. Design a leaflet encouraging him or her to join one group. Write no more than 20 words on this leaflet.

What opposition did Suffragettes and Suffragists face?

When the Liberal government came to power in 1906, many women hoped that electoral reform would soon follow. However, this did not happen. In the early 1900s many MPs and most people were against giving the **franchise** to women. Some people did not think that giving women the vote was an important issue; others were afraid of the changes that would result if women could vote. Indeed, many women did not want the right to vote – they thought that political matters should be left to men.

Key words

Franchise The right to vote.

SOURCE E

In 1889 Mrs Humphrey Ward, a successful novelist, published an anti-suffragist petition that was presented to Parliament. Women who opposed the suffrage campaign argued that women could have more influence through their own individual efforts, or through their social role as hostesses, than the right to vote would give them.

From a modern history textbook.

SOURCE F

Male doctors were prepared to argue that women were unsuited for the world of politics since they were too emotional and prone to mental unrest. A doctor's letter to *The Times* in 1912 reads: 'these upsettings of her mental equilibrium are the things that a woman has most cause to fear; and no doctor can ever lose sight of the fact that the mind of woman is always threatened with danger'.

An historian writing in 2001.

AN "UGLY RUSH!"

MR. BULL. "NOT IF I KNOW IT!"   [See Division on the Woman's Vote Bill.

A contemporary Punch cartoon, 'An Ugly Rush!' The man
blocking the door to women's political rights is 'John Bull' –
he represents the general British attitude.

💡 What do you think is the message of Source G?

💡 Who do you think the women standing quietly in the
background are?

The violent actions of the Suffragettes succeeded in gaining
publicity for their cause, but they probably did more harm than
good. Although there was more public interest in the issue of votes
for women, the Suffragettes failed to win public support and the
government became more reluctant to acknowledge their views.
Although the Suffragettes claimed that they would never cause
physical harm to another person, the damage they inflicted on
property and their aggressive methods turned many people
against them.

Hunger strikes and forced feeding

Some Suffragettes had been put in prison for their protests. In 1909 a Suffragette who had been imprisoned decided to go on **hunger strike**. The government did not want the Suffragettes to have a martyr, so it put a stop to the strike by releasing her. However, others carried on this protest.

Key words

Hunger strike A protest involving someone refusing to eat.

In an attempt to stop the Suffragettes from using hunger strikes, the government decided to introduce a policy of forced feeding. Women on hunger strike were force-fed through a two-metre-long rubber tube that was pushed down the throat and into the stomach. Lime cordial and meat juice were then passed through the tube. This was an unpleasant procedure and the Suffragettes created posters to win sympathy for their treatment (see Source H). The poster campaign was very effective and eventually King George V asked the government to stop its policy of forced feeding.

SOURCE H

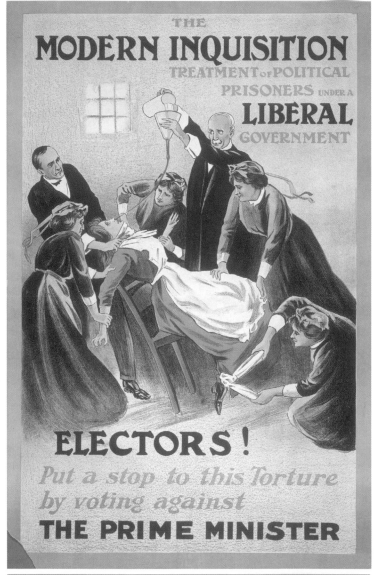

The front cover of the Suffragette journal, **Votes for Women**, in 1910.

💡 What five questions would you like to ask to find out more about Source H? Use the 5Ws to help you. (Why? What? When? Who? Where?)

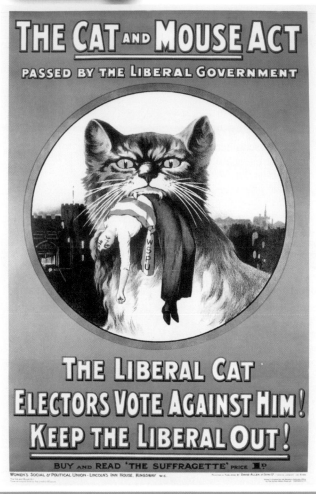

A Suffragette poster of 1913 about the 'Cat and Mouse Act'.

The 'Cat and Mouse Act'

The government had to find a way to treat Suffragettes on hunger strike humanely *and* keep them in prison. In 1913 the government therefore passed an Act to release women who starved themselves from prison. On release, the women had to agree to certain conditions and could be re-arrested and put back in prison once their health improved. This new Act quickly became known as the 'Cat and Mouse Act'.

TASKS...

1 Look at Source I.
   a) Who does the cat represent? How is the cat portrayed?
   b) Who does the woman represent? How is she portrayed?
   c) What message does this poster give about the 'Cat and Mouse Act'?
   d) Can we trust the message of the poster? Give reasons for your answer.

2 Look at Sources H and I on this page and page 74.
   a) What do you think these images tell us about the opposition that women's suffrage movements faced?
   b) Do you think we can trust these two images to tell the truth about the opposition that women's suffrage groups faced? Explain your answer using the images and other information from this section.

How did the women's suffrage movement finally succeed?

All women over 21 were given the vote.

'Votes for Women'

1928

1916

Women over 30 who were householders or wives of householders were given the vote, as were graduates.

1918

Voting laws had to be changed when men went off to war, so that an election could take place. All men were now allowed to vote. David Lloyd George, who supported women's suffrage, was elected as prime minister.

1914: First World War breaks out
Suffragists and Suffragettes end their political campaigns. They take on men's jobs while they are away fighting. This shows the government that they are capable and responsible.

1914

TASKS...

Look at the 'hurdles' above.

1 Which event do you think was most important in helping women to gain the vote? Explain your decision.

2 Look at your living graph and diary planner.
   a) Plot the impact of electoral reform in 1918 and 1928 on your living graph.
   b) In your diary planner explain where you have placed the characters on the graph and why.

Plenary

💡 Which event do you think has had the greatest impact on electoral reform? Give reasons for your answer.

💡 What arguments might you give to explain why voting is so important in today's society? Give examples of countries where there is not a democracy. What problems do you think people living in these areas face?

💡 71 per cent of the population voted in the 1997 general election. This figure fell to 59 per cent in the 2001 general election. Why do you think so few people vote nowadays?

REVOLUTIONS: WAS THE PERIOD FROM 1750 TO 1900 AN ERA OF PROGRESS?

Conclusion

In this chapter you have studied a number of different 'revolutions'. You have considered how people reacted to these 'revolutions' and how their lives changed as a result of them. Now it is time to decide whether the period 1750 to 1900 was an era of progress. To do this, think about the situation in 1750 and the situation by 1900. How much progress do you think there had been?

TASKS...

1   Give each 'revolution' a score on a sliding scale of 10 to minus 10. Here are some guidelines to help you with your scoring.
   • A score of 10 means a great deal of progress had been made (progress).
   • A score of 5 means some progress had been made (progress).
   • A score of 0 means no progress had been made.
   • A score of minus 5 means that life had got worse as a result of the changes (regress).
   • A score of minus 10 means had got *much* worse as a result of the changes (regress).

2   Copy and complete the chart below. Use the score you gave each 'revolution' to decide how much of each column you need to shade.

	Agriculture	Industry	Working conditions	Transport	The Vote
10					
5					
0					
-5					
-10					

3   Now answer the question: *'How far was the period 1750 to 1900 an age of progress?'* Explain your answer carefully.

THEME: RIGHTS AND FREEDOMS

INTRODUCTION

💡 How 'free' are you? In small groups think about:

- things you are free to do
- how you would react if your freedom was taken away

- things you are free from
- how you might try to get your freedom back.

Share you ideas with the rest of the class.

In the next few chapters you will examine how certain groups of people throughout history have had their rights and freedoms limited and how they reacted to this. Before you begin, think about what types of rights and freedoms have been denied to some people in the past…

💡 Look at the timeline below and Sources A to E. What does this information tell you about the rights and freedoms that have been denied people between 1750–1990?

💡 What methods might these people have used to gain their freedom? Make a note of your ideas – you will re-visit them at the end of this section.

TIMELINE
Rights and freedoms, 1750–1964

1709	Slave traders set out on their first voyage from Liverpool to buy and sell slaves.
1833	While India is part of the British Empire, the educational system is introduced in India to teach the English language to native children.
1857	The Indian Mutiny: when the British are disrespectful of Indian religious beliefs there is a violent rebellion against British involvement in India.
1890	The Jim Crow Laws: black Americans are forced to live totally separate lives from white Americans.
1938	*Kristallnacht* (the Night of the Broken Glass) – a night of violence against German Jews.
1939	All Jews in Poland have to wear a yellow star, which easily identifies them.
1942	The Final Solution is put in place by the Nazis; this results in the murder of approximately six million European Jews.
1947	India becomes independent from British rule.
1964	Martin Luther King, a leading Civil Rights campaigner in the USA, wins the Nobel Peace Prize.

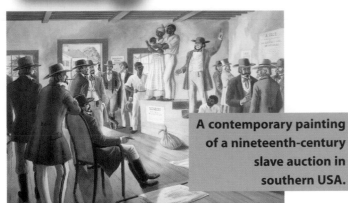

SOURCE A

A contemporary painting of a nineteenth-century slave auction in southern USA.

SOURCE B

A photograph of separation of black people from white people in the USA in the early twentieth century.

SOURCE C

A photograph of Indian troops in France fighting for Britain during the First World War.

SOURCE D

A photograph of a Jewish mother and her children in the Warsaw Ghetto, Poland, 1943.

A photograph of Jews being taken to a concentration camp during the Second World War (1942).

SOURCE E

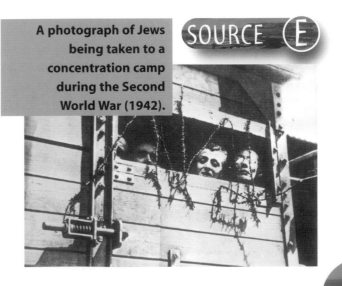

FROM SLAVERY TO CIVIL RIGHTS: WHAT WAS THE BLACK PERSON'S EXPERIENCE OF THE UNITED STATES OF AMERICA?

WHAT WAS THE SLAVE TRADE?

Objectives

In this section you will find out:
- how slaves were captured and transported to the Americas
- what conditions were like on the 'Middle Passage'.

To investigate these ideas you will:
- assess a variety of sources
- produce an account of a slave's experience of capture and transportation.

Starter
Read Source A.

SOURCE A

Kunta wondered if he had gone mad. Naked, chained, shackled, he awoke on his back between two other men in a pitch darkness full of steamy heat and sickening stink and a nightmarish bedlam of shrieking, weeping, praying and vomiting. He could feel and smell his own vomit on his chest and belly. His whole body was one spasm of pain from the beatings he had received in the four days since his capture. But the place where the hot iron had been put between his shoulders hurt the worst.

A rat's thick, furry body brushed his cheek, sniffing at his mouth. In a rage, Kunta snatched and kicked against the shackles that bound his wrists and ankles. He felt himself starting to vomit again and he tried to force it back, but couldn't. His already emptied belly squeezed up a thin, sour fluid that drained from the side of his mouth as he lay wishing that he might die.

After a while he very slowly and carefully explored his shackled right wrist and ankle. They were bleeding. He seemed to be connected by the left ankle and wrist to some other man. They were all so close that their shoulders, arms and legs touched if any of them moved even a little. There wasn't enough space even to sit up.

As Kunta lay listening, he slowly began to realise that he was trying to push from his mind the impulse to relieve the demands of his bowels, which he had been forcing back for days. But he could hold it in no longer, and finally the faeces curled out between his buttocks.

Revolted at himself, smelling his own addition to the stench, Kunta began sobbing and again his belly gave a spasm. What sins was he being punished for in such a manner as this? He pleaded to Allah for an answer.

From Alex Haley's book Roots (1976).

Alex Haley was an African American author who traced his family roots back to their African origins. Source A gives a short extract from his book.

💡 *What questions would you like to ask to find out more about the story of Kunta?*

Record your ideas on a copy of the question wheel opposite. Think about what makes a good question and what you need to find out about Kunta.

Share your questions with the class and your reasons for choosing them. As a class, decide on the six best questions. As you work through this section, try to find the answers to your questions.

What does it mean to be a slave?

A slave is a person owned by someone else; a piece of property. Slavery has occurred many times in history. It existed in the great civilisations of Egypt, Greece and Rome. Rulers and armies of these empires would often make prisoners of war their slaves. After the fall of the Roman Empire in the fifth century CE, slavery became less common. One place where it did continue was Africa. Before the arrival of white Europeans in Africa, people were made slaves for a number of reasons.

- Many people were captured during battles between tribes. They would be kept as slaves until a ransom was paid for their freedom.

- Some people were enslaved as a punishment for committing crime.

- Some people agreed to become slaves to escape poverty and starvation, particularly during times of famine or drought.

- People were also sold to Arab slave dealers in return for luxury goods.

The treatment of slaves in Africa varied from tribe to tribe. In many instances, people were able to escape from their slavery.

However, the slave trade changed when white Europeans became involved after 1440. It became international and made huge profits for those involved. More importantly, slavery became a way of life from which there was no escape. Children of slaves became slaves themselves. The Portuguese were the first Europeans to become involved in the slave trade. However, Britain and other European countries followed, and began shipping slaves from Africa to sell abroad for profit.

Why did the Europeans need slaves?

By the late fifteenth century European countries such as Portugal, Spain, France and Britain had acquired **colonies** in **the Americas**. Europeans needed workers to build settlements and farm the land. At first the local population was used, but many died of European diseases. These **natives** needed to be replaced and so Europeans looked towards Africa to provide a slave labour force.

In **the 'New World'**, these African slaves were used to clear and farm new land. Others were used as servants or as skilled craftsmen making things like jewellery and leather goods. A 'triangular' trade eventually developed. The map below explains how this trade worked.

> ### Key words
>
> **Colonies** Countries ruled by another country.
>
> **The Americas** North and South America and the islands close by.
>
> **Natives** Local inhabitants of a country or area.
>
> **The New World** The name given to North and South America and the islands close by after their discovery in 1492.

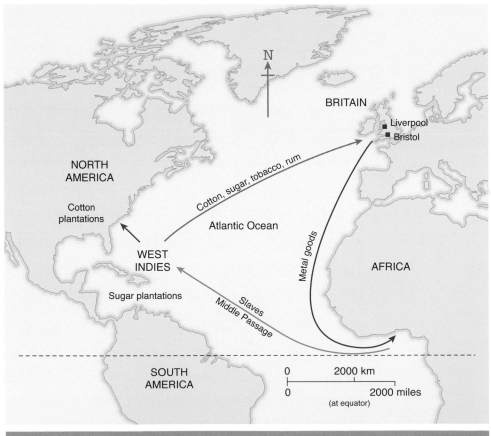

A map showing the triangular trade.

TASKS…

1 Do you agree with the following statements? Explain why or why not.

- Slavery began only in the sixteenth century.
- Only black Africans were slaves.
- There were many reasons for slavery.
- Slaves were used for many different jobs.

What happened to slaves on the middle passage?

TASKS…

1 At the end of this section you will begin a 'slave diary' in which you describe and explain your experiences of capture and the voyage to the Americas. (You will complete this diary at the end of the next section.) To help you write your diary, copy and complete the following planning sheet. You will add to this planning sheet in the next section, so be sure you leave enough space in your book.

	Characters	Ideas for your diary
Capture		
Transportation		

How were slaves captured?

Africans themselves were involved in the slave trade. It was unusual for the slave traders to get the slaves they needed by kidnapping Africans from coastal villages, so they did deals with African chiefs who organised the collection of slaves. These chiefs often carried out raids inland. Slaves were then exchanged for goods such as alcohol, cloth, metals, jewellery and guns. Once slaves had been transported to the coast, they were kept in forts called 'barracoons'. They were often chained by the neck or legs before being shipped across the Atlantic Ocean to their destinations.

One day, when the adults were out working and my sister and I were left to mind the house, two men and a woman got over our wall. They seized us both and ran off with us to the nearest wood. In the morning, we left the wood and took to a road. I saw some people in the distance and called out for help, but my captors tied me up and stuffed me in a sack.

The next day my sister and I were separated. I was sold here and there, then moved on. After about seven months we reached the coast. The first thing I saw was the sea and a slave ship, anchored, waiting for its cargo. I was taken on board and handled roughly by the crew to see if I was healthy. Their skin was a different colour from ours.

From Olaudah Equiano's autobiographical story, *The interesting narrative of the life of Olaudah Equiano*, written in 1789. Equiano eventually bought his freedom and settled in Britain. He became an anti-slavery campaigner.

What happened during transportation?

The journey from Africa to the Americas became known as the Middle Passage. This journey took between six and twelve weeks, depending on the weather. The aim of each ship's captain was to keep alive as many slaves as possible because only those who survived the journey could be sold. Sources C to G highlight what often happened during these voyages.

SOURCE **C**   SOURCE **D**

Below deck, the stench and crying made me so sick and low that I wanted to die. I was severely beaten. I would have jumped overboard but we were being watched carefully. Two of my countrymen who were chained together somehow made it through the netting and jumped into the sea. Many more would have done the same if they had not been stopped by the ship's crew.

I had never seen before such brutal cruelty. One man was flogged so mercilessly that he died and was tossed over the side as they would have done a brute. The heat [and the overcrowding] almost suffocated us. The air became unfit to breathe and brought on a sickness among the slaves. Many died.

Written by Olaudah Equiano in 1789.

About 8 am, slaves were generally brought up on deck. If the weather was good they would remain chained on deck until mid-afternoon. Their food was served in large tubs. About ten slaves would eat from the same tub using wooden spoons.

Those who wouldn't eat were punished. One captain poured molten lead on slaves, while another captain burnt slaves' lips by placing shovels of hot coals close to their mouths.

Written by a modern historian.

SOURCE E

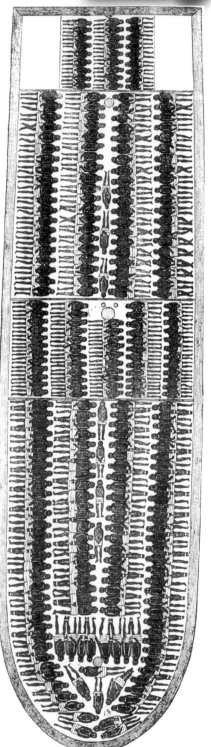

The Brookes was a slave ship originally built to carry a maximum of 450 people. But in 1788 it was found to be carrying 609 slaves.

💡 The image of the slave ship shown in Source E was used by **abolitionists** (see pages 95–6). Why do you think it is such a powerful image? Is it likely to be accurate?

Key words

Abolitionists People who thought that slavery was wrong and should be stopped. They often campaigned for this cause.

SOURCE F

Every slave, whatever his size, was found to have only five feet and six inches [about 1.7 metres] in length and sixteen inches [about 40 centimetres] in breadth to lie in. The floor was covered with bodies packed according to this allowance. But between the floor and deck were often platforms that were also covered with bodies. The men were chained two and two together by their hands and feet. Their allowance consisted of one pint of water a day each. They were fed twice a day with yams and horse beans.

Written by Thomas Clarkson in a nineteenth-century history book.

SOURCE G

The situation was aggravated by the rubbing of the chains and filth of the lavatory-buckets into which the children often fell. The shrieks of women and the groans of the dying rendered the whole a scene of horror.

On many of the ships the sense of misery was so terrible slaves would often go mad before dying of suffocation. In their frenzy some killed others, in the hope of getting more room to breathe. Men strangled those next to them and women drove nails into each other's brains. So many dead people were thrown overboard on slave ships that sharks would pick up a ship off the coast of Africa and follow it to America.

Written by Olaudah Equiano in 1789.

TASKS...

Imagine it is 1788. You have been taken from your home by a raiding party and sold into slavery. You sailed aboard the *Brookes* slave ship (shown in Source E). Write a diary of your recent experiences, using the diary planning sheet you completed on page 83 and Sources C to G to help you with the details.

Write two entries in your diary.
- In the first entry, introduce yourself. Describe your capture.
- In the second entry, describe your experiences aboard the *Brookes* slave ship. It would be a good idea to have separate paragraphs on food, punishment, conditions below deck and what happened on deck.

Remember, this diary will need to be written in the first person using the past tense to describe what has happened to you. Use connectives to link together the main points you make in your paragraphs.

Plenary

Most of the sources you have read about the Middle Passage are critical of the slave trade. How do you think the authors have communicated this?

WHAT WAS LIFE LIKE FOR SLAVES ON A PLANTATION?

Objectives

In this section you will find out:
- how slaves were sold in the Americas
- how hard life was for slaves on plantations.

To investigate these ideas you will:
- examine a variety of sources
- produce a written account of a slave's experience of plantation life.

Starter

Read the following slave laws.

💡 *What do you think would be the purpose of each of these laws? Discuss this with other members of your class.*

Key words

Testimonies Evidence given by witnesses in a trial.

Branded Burnt with a hot iron to leave an identifiable mark.

Plantations Large farms on which slaves grew crops such as cotton or tobacco.

- *Husbands may be sold from their wives.*
- *Children may be sold from their mothers.*
- *Slaves are not to be taught to read and write.*
- *Slaves cannot own property.*
- *Slave **testimonies** cannot be used in court against white people.*
- *Slaves are not allowed to travel.*
- *Slaves caught trying to run away will be **branded** with an iron.*
- *Slaves cannot gather together in groups.*
- *Slaves cannot carry weapons.*

How were slaves sold?

Slaves who survived the horrors of the Middle Passage would usually be sold to **plantation** owners. Before their arrival in the Americas, slaves would often have oil rubbed onto their skin to hide signs of illness and to make them look healthy.

Once the ship had arrived, slaves were most commonly sold through auction. At the auction, slaves went to the highest bidder (the person who offered the most money). Interested buyers would be allowed to examine the slaves.

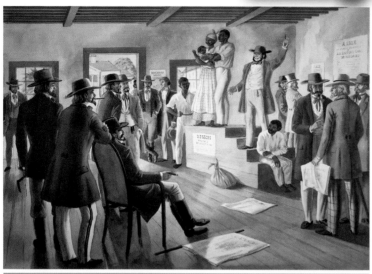

A slave auction in nineteenth-century America.

Families were often split up and sold separately at auction. Once slaves were bought they were usually branded and taken to plantations or farms to work.

💡 What do you think the slaves would have been thinking in Source A?

Plantation life for slaves: the evidence

TASKS...

1 Look back at your 'slave diary'. At the end of this section you will write the final entry in this diary to describe and explain your experiences of being sold at a slave auction and of life on a plantation. To help you write your diary, continue using your planning sheet by adding new sections – as the example below shows.

	Characters	Ideas for your diary
Capture		
Transportation		
Arrival		
Plantation life		

Most black people were slaves on plantations. These plantations grew a variety of crops such as coffee, tobacco and sugar. In the southern states of America, most plantations grew cotton. In 1793 the USA produced 10,000 bales of cotton. By 1800 it was producing 100,000 bales, most of which was sold in England. On cotton plantations, slaves were used to plant and look after the crops, then harvest them.

The slaves had to work long hours under the blazing hot sun. Often, children as young as six would be forced to work in the fields. At the end of the working day slaves would go back to their living quarters. In some cases, these were no more than hovels (see Source C).

Some slaves were sold to **masters** who treated them reasonably well. However, some owners had a reputation for cruelty. The power of the masters over their slaves was almost unlimited. Even the 'best' slave owners sometimes used the whip to punish their slaves. But in some cases the brutality was much worse.

SOURCE B

The cotton picking season begins at the end of August. The workers have to be in the cotton field as soon as it is light in the morning. You have ten minutes to swallow your dinner of cold bacon. You are not permitted to be a minute idle until it is too dark to see. When the moon is full, you must work till the middle of the night.

Solomon Northop writing in his autobiography, *Twelve Years A Slave* (1847).

SOURCE C

In a single room were huddled, like cattle, ten or twelve men, women and children. There were neither bedsteads nor furniture. Our beds were collections of straw and old rags. The wind whistled, and the rain and snow blew in through the cracks. The earth floor soaked in the moisture till it was just like a pigsty.

A slave, Josiah Henson, describes his experiences on a plantation, 1849.

SOURCE D

Flogging of up to 75 lashes was common. On many occasions, planters branded, stabbed, **tarred and feathered**, burned, shackled, tortured, maimed, crippled, mutilated and castrated their slaves. Thousands of slaves were flogged so badly that they were permanently scarred.

Written by a modern historian.

SOURCE E

Key words

Master The owner of the slave.

Tarred and feathered Smeared with tar and then covered with feathers as a punishment.

A contemporary drawing of a slave being punished by a beating.

Africans are nothing but brutes. They will love you better for whipping, whether they deserve it or not.

A plantation owner in the nineteenth century describes how he treats his slaves.

None of the evils of slavery are more horrible than the treatment of females. They were obliged to give in to prostitution, to equal labour with males and to become the breeders of slaves at the will and pleasure of their masters.

From the journal of Major J.B. Colthurst, published in 1847. Colthurst was a special judge sent to the Caribbean from Britain.

Again and again the whip fell on his back. His cries grew fainter, until a feeble groan was all you heard. His head was then put against a post and his right ear was nailed to it. A sharp knife was used to cut off his ear and leave it sticking to the post.

Josiah Henson describes how his father was punished for protecting his mother against the sexual advances of the plantation overseer.

What impression of plantation owners do you gain from Sources D to H?

TASKS...

1 What can you learn about the hardships of plantation life from Sources B and C?

2 Do Sources D, G and H agree or disagree with Source E? Explain your answer carefully.

3 Use your diary planning sheet, which you completed on page 88, to write the final entry in your slave diary about life on the plantations. It would be a good idea to have separate paragraphs about being sold at auction, the jobs done on a plantation, the living conditions and the punishment from slave owners.

Plenary

Read Source I. If you had to give five reasons to support the source, what would they be?

How do you think a plantation owner might respond to this criticism?

The white people have robbed us for centuries. They have made Africa bleed rivers of blood! They have torn husbands from wives, parents from children, sisters from brothers and bound them in chains.

David Ruggles, a black bookseller from New York, speaking in 1834.

FIGHTING FOR THEIR FREEDOM: HOW DID SLAVES RESIST ENSLAVEMENT?

Objectives

In this section you will find out:
- how slavery was resisted
- how successful the resistance was.

To investigate these ideas you will:
- use sources to reach a reasoned conclusion
- produce a piece of writing that shows your understanding.

Starter

Imagine a school assembly where the head teacher announces the following measures to take immediate effect.

- *There will be a 50 per cent increase in the amount of homework set.*
- *An extra lesson will be added on to the school day.*
- *All extra-curricular clubs will stop.*

Key words

Legitimate Lawful or legal.

*In small groups, think of the **legitimate** ways you could resist these measures. When you have done this, choose the five methods most likely to work. List them in order of how successful you think they would be.*

Now share your ideas with the rest of the class. What were the most popular methods of resistance? How likely would they be to succeed?

Now repeat the exercise, but this time consider what slaves could do to resist slavery. Share your ideas with the rest of the class. Was this second list harder to come up with? Suggest why this might be.

How was slavery resisted?

Wherever there was slavery, it was resisted. This resistance took many forms. Some were more dramatic than others. Some had more success than others.

TASKS...

1 Copy the chart below into your book. You will fill in this chart as you work through this section, so make sure you leave yourself plenty of room. **WS**

Statement	Evidence to support the statement	Evidence to contradict the statement	Does the statement need changing? If so how?
Passive resistance by slaves was successful.			
Slave rebellions never succeeded.			
Peaceful resistance to slavery was more successful than the use of violence.			

Passive resistance

Slaves often used non-violent, or passive, methods to resist slavery. These included working slowly, doing work badly, deliberately damaging things like tools and crops, and pretending to be ill. These methods cut down the profits made by plantation owners and could result in slaves being punished if caught.

Escape

Some slaves tried to run away. If caught, the punishment for this was likely to be having the letter 'R' branded on the cheek or the removal of an ear.

💡 Why do you think runaway slaves would be punished in this way?

In the USA some runaway slaves were helped by a secret organisation called the Underground Railroad. This organisation was run by white people in the northern states, and provided a system of safe houses (known as stations) where escaping slaves could hide during daylight hours.

One of the most famous conductors (people who led slaves from one station to another) was Harriet Tubman (see Source A). She had escaped from slavery in the south when she was 29. Harriet made another nineteen trips to the south during her lifetime, leading 300 slaves to freedom in Canada.

Slave owners offered a reward of US$40,000 for Harriet – dead or alive. But she was never caught. Harriet was one of about 3000 people who risked their lives to help slaves to freedom.

Because the Underground Railroad was a secret organisation there is very little evidence about it. However, it is thought that about 50,000 slaves were helped to escape to freedom.

💡 In 1886, the writer Sarah Bradford called Harriet Tubman the 'Moses' of her people. Why do you think she called her this?

WANTED

HARRIET TUBMAN

$40,000 REWARD

Harriet Tubman.

Rebellion

Slaves preferred not to rebel because often they would be brutally crushed by slave owners who were frightened by the idea of a slave revolt. Most slave rebellions did not succeed. But the Amistad revolt did.

The Amistad revolt

The slave trade had been abolished in stages. In 1807 Britain and the USA banned international trade in slaves. Spain did the same in 1820. Despite this ban, the trade in slaves continued illegally.

SOURCE B

Cinque, painted in about 1840.

In Cuba in April 1839, Joseph Cinque and 53 other Africans were sold to two Spaniards, Ruiz and Montes, for their plantation. They were loaded onto the illegal slave ship, *Amistad*, in Havana. While still in port, Cinque led a rebellion. The ship's cook and captain were killed and the rest of the crew were set adrift in a small boat. The slaves ordered Ruiz and Montes to sail them back to Africa. However, *Amistad* sailed towards the North American coast and was eventually captured in November by the US navy. Cinque and the other slaves were arrested for murder.

By the time the trial started in January 1840, seventeen of the slaves had died in prison. The surviving Africans argued that they were free men who were being held captive. The jury agreed with them, and the judge set the Africans free.

Opponents of the decision appealed, and the President of the USA, Van Buren, demanded the case be heard by the **Supreme Court**. This was held in March 1841. The former president, John Quincy Adams, defended the slaves. The Supreme Court agreed with the earlier decision. In January 1842, Cinque and the other surviving Africans arrived in the West African country of Sierra Leone as free men.

Key words

Supreme Court The most important court in the USA.

TASKS...

1 Either:

   a) Write a summing up statement for the barrister prosecuting the Amistad slaves in the Supreme Court in 1841.

   b) Write a summing up statement for John Quincy Adams who defended the Amistad slaves. Use the following guidelines to help you write your statement.

   • Begin with a powerful opening statement about what decision the Supreme Court should reach on this case. Explain how your opponent will try to influence the court. For each argument you give explain why it is not convincing. Then put forward each of the main arguments supporting your case. Back up each one with evidence. End your statement with a conclusion, in which you state what the dire consequences of agreeing with your opponent would be and what the consequences of agreeing with your view would be.

   • Write your statement in the first person and present tense. Use connectives that are related to logic and persuasion such as *in fact, because, therefore, however, obviously, importantly, clearly, surely, undoubtedly*.

EXTENSION TASK...

2 Find out whether or not the rebellions led by Toussaint L'Overture in San Domingo in the 1790s and Nat Turner in Virginia in 1831 were successful.

Plenary

Write down the five most important or interesting pieces of information you have learned in this section. Share your choices with the rest of the class. What were the similarities and differences in the choices you made?

ABOLITION AND EMANCIPATION: WHAT WERE THE RESULTS?

Objectives

In this section you will find out:

- the changes that took place in the lives of black Americans after **emancipation** in 1865
- the impact these changes had on their lives.

To investigate these ideas you will:

- assess whether emancipation led to an improvement in the lives of black Americans
- produce a living graph and a piece of extended writing.

Starter

Take a look at Sources A and B.

SOURCE A

Does not God love coloured children as well as white children? And did not the same Saviour die to save the one as well as the other? If so, white children must know that if they go to heaven, they must go without their **prejudice** against colour, for in heaven black and white are one in the love of Jesus. Get rid of your prejudice and learn to love coloured children that you may be all the children of your father who is in heaven.

From a speech by Sojourner Truth in 1863.

Key words

Prejudice A narrow-minded view based on insufficient knowledge.

Providence Divine intention.

Emancipation Freedom.

SOURCE B

We need answer only to God for slavery. And slavery clearly has His blessing. Black Africans are destined by **providence** to slavery. They are in all respects inferior to us. They are not able to cope with freedom. People only have to look to Africa to see how much slaves have gained by their servitude.

The views of George McDuffie, the Governor of South Carolina from 1834–6.

- *Which of these sources do you think was spoken by a supporter of slavery, and which was spoken by an abolitionist?*
- *How do the people speaking in the sources justify their viewpoint?*
- *Which do you find the most powerful statement – Source A or Source B? Explain why.*

Share your ideas with others in the class.

A debate over whether or not slavery should be abolished raged for many years. By 1858 nineteen northern states of the USA had become 'free' states – states where slavery had been abolished. In these states an abolition movement was set up to campaign for an end to slavery. White abolitionists such as William Lloyd Garrison and Harriet Beecher Stowe and black abolitionists such as Frederick Douglass and Sojourner Truth used many different tactics to get publicity for their cause. They wrote pamphlets, made speeches, published their own newspapers, preached in churches and even set up schools.

TASKS...

Find out more about the tactics these abolitionists used to campaign for the abolition of slavery in the USA.

In the southern states of the USA the abolition movement was resented. Plantation owners were unwilling to end slavery because it provided them with a free labour force. Many white Americans had justified slavery by thinking of slaves as racially inferior, as people without human needs, rights or dignity. The legal system had supported these racist views, and the rights of the plantation owners, for many years.

Tension between North and South increased. The election of Abraham Lincoln as president in 1860 was the final straw. He had spoken out against slavery many times. Eleven southern slave owning states decided to leave the USA and form a new country – The Confederate States of America. Lincoln could not allow this to happen so in April 1861 the USA was plunged into a bloody civil war between the Union, or Northern states, and the Confederacy.

The defeat of the Confederacy in April 1865 led to the following changes to the **American Constitution**:

- the 13th **Amendment** (December 1865), in which slavery was abolished

- the 14th Amendment (1866), in which black Americans were given full citizenship of the USA

- the 15th Amendment (1870), in which black and white men were given equal voting rights.

But did this mean that black people were really free?

Key words

American Constitution A document which states the legal rights of all Americans.

Amendment A correction made with the approval of the government.

TASKS...

1 As you work through the material on pages 97–100 you will need to create information cards that will be used on page 100 to complete a living graph. This graph will show whether the lives of black people improved after the emancipation proclamation (statement of freedom) in 1865.

For each theme, complete your cards by deciding how much improvement there was for black people after 1865. Give each theme covered a score out of 10, as follows.

- A score of 10 means there was a definite improvement.
- A score of 5 to 9 means there was some improvement, but there were still difficulties faced by black Americans.
- A score of 1 to 4 means there was little real improvement, though some change.
- A score of 0 means there was no improvement.
  For each score, explain why you came to that decision.

Theme:

Score out of 10:

Reason for decision:

Theme 1: Legal rights

By 1870 black Americans had been given the following rights by law.

- Equal **civil rights**.

- The right to vote and to stand for election.

- The right to sit on juries and become judges.

- The right to legally own land.

- The right to marry and have children without the fear of being separated from their families.

In the south, where racial hatred remained a problem, black people's new rights were protected by northern soldiers who remained after the Civil War. When these soldiers left in 1877, many **state governments** chose to persecute black people and limit their rights. Despite the laws of the **federal government**, they soon took away black people's rights to vote.

Key words

Civil rights The rights of each citizen to political and social equality and freedom.

State government Government responsible for each state's internal affairs.

Federal government The central government based in Washington, responsible for national issues.

Theme 2: the Freedman's Bureau

At the end of the civil war a Freedman's Bureau was set up to tackle the problems freed slaves might face. This bureau opened more than 4000 free schools, which educated about 250,000 black students. The bureau also established health care facilities, set up orphanages and helped former slaves to find work.

The Freedman's Bureau helped to improve literacy among black people. By 1870, 21 per cent of black people in the south could read. However, after 1877 many schools for black people were forced to close by white racists. Some schools were burned and students were beaten up.

Theme 3: Sharecropping

Sharecropping was introduced by southern landowners because they no longer had slaves to work their land. Under the system, free black people worked for a share of the crops – usually about one-third (although from this they had to buy tools and supplies from landowners' shops). The southern landowners still owned the land and many black sharecroppers ended up working for their old masters, but as free people. The system of sharecropping relied on good harvests. But many sharecroppers spent more than their share was worth and fell heavily into debt.

Sharecroppers at work on a plantation in the 1860s.

Theme 4: The Ku Klux Klan

In the years following the Civil War, terrorist groups such as the White League and the Ku Klux Klan (KKK) were formed. The KKK was set up as a secret society. Its aim was to make sure that white people controlled society by terrifying black people and ethnic minorities.

The Klan used brutal violence. Black people were beaten, **lynched**, burned, shot or drowned. Employees of the Freedman's Bureau and white northern teachers, who educated black people, were also threatened. The KKK was banned in 1872 but it continued illegally and was popular. Judges and policeman were often Klan members, so it was difficult to stop the Klan's activities.

Key words

Lynch To judge and put to death without a legal trial.

SOURCE

A cartoon from *Harper's Weekly* about the terrorist groups, the White League and the Ku Klux Klan, 1874.

💡 Why do you think the Ku Klux Klan became so popular in the southern states?

Theme 5: Segregation

After 1890 many southern governments passed a series of laws that set up a system of segregation that would last until the mid-twentieth century. This system meant that black people were forced to live separately from white people. They were given separate places on buses, in theatres, in hospitals and in churches. Black children were forced to attend different schools to white children. Public benches, toilets and water fountains were labelled for use by 'white people' or by 'coloured' people.

Violence was often used to enforce the system of segregation. More than 2000 people were lynched or burned in the last two decades of the nineteenth century. Southern newspapers would advertise these executions, and even children would be taken to lynchings. People had their photographs taken with the victims.

SOURCE E

A photograph to show the segregation of black people in the USA, early twentieth century.

These two men, Thomas Shipp and Abram Smith, had been accused of murdering a white man and dragged from jail by a lynch mob, 1930.

SOURCE G

Southern trees bear a strange fruit,
Blood on the leaves and blood at the root,
Black bodies swingin' in the southern breeze,
Strange fruit from the poplar trees.

An extract from a song by the black jazz musician, Billie Holliday, 1939.

TASKS...

1 Copy a larger version of this graph into your book. Plot the scores from the information cards you have been keeping on your graph. **WS**

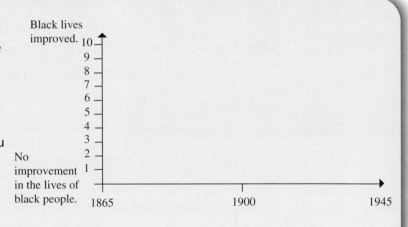

2 Now study your graph. Do you think life had improved for black Americans by 1900? Explain your decision to the rest of the class.

3 'The abolition of slavery was a success. It brought about an improvement in the lives of black people by the beginning of the twentieth century.'

Write an essay to explain whether you agree with this interpretation. Use the findings from your graph to help you write your answer. **WS**

Plenary

Look at Source G. Popular songs are often used to give a particular message. What point is Billie Holliday trying to make in this song? Have a go at writing the next verse. It must be based on what you have learned about the experiences of black Americans from 1865 to 1900. Share your ideas with others in the class.

HOW SUCCESSFUL WAS THE CAMPAIGN FOR CIVIL RIGHTS IN THE TWENTIETH CENTURY?

Objectives

In this section you will find out:
- the problems that black Americans faced in the 1940s and 50s
- whether the Civil Rights Movement was a success.
- the effect of Martin Luther King on the Civil Rights Movement.

To investigate these ideas you will:
- summarise success and failure using a range of evidence
- create a game based upon the Civil Rights Movement
- produce a documentary on the life of Martin Luther King.

Starter

Look at Sources A and B.

 SOURCE A

A photograph of a bus station waiting room showing segregation in the late 1950s.

 SOURCE B

A black man is kicked by a crowd of white men, 1943.

- *What do these photographs tell you about the problems faced by black people in the 1940s and 1950s?*
- *What other problems do you think Sources A and B suggest?*
- *What do you think are the uses and limitations of using photographs as evidence of the problems facing black Americans in the 1940s and 1950s?*

What was life like for black Americans in the first half of the twentieth century?

There was little improvement in the lives of black Americans during the first half of the twentieth century. Some organisations were set up to fight for the rights of black Americans. The National Association for the Advancement of Coloured People (NAACP) was established by William Du Bois in 1909. Its aims were the abolition of segregation, and equal voting and educational opportunities for black Americans. The Universal Negro Improvement Association (UNIA) was established by Marcus Garvey in 1914 with similar aims, but had little success.

Black Americans did not share in the economic prosperity of the 1920s. They were also among the hardest hit during the severe economic depression of the 1930s, and they failed to benefit from President Roosevelt's 'New Deal' which attempted to improve the lives of Americans.

SOURCE C

WORLD'S HIGHEST STANDARD OF LIVING

There's no way like the American Way

Black Americans queue for food handouts during the Depression, 1937.

💡 Can you explain the **irony** in Source C?

Black soldiers fought in segregated units in both the First World War (1914–18) and the Second World War (1939–45). When these wars ended, tension increased as black and white soldiers returning home competed for jobs and housing. After 1945, there was a renewed determination among black people to bring about an end to segregation, **discrimination**, poverty and violence against black people.

Key words

Discrimination Unfair treatment because of race, religion or sex.

Irony A humourous use of words in which the intended meaning is the opposite of what is actually said.

When did the Civil Rights Movement begin?

In the 1950s a Civil Rights Movement began to emerge. It campaigned for an end to segregation. It also fought for black people to have:

- the right to take part in government (including the right to vote in elections)
- an equal standard of health care
- an equal standard of education
- an equal protection by the law.

Read through the key events of the Civil Rights Movement below. For each one, think about:

- whether it was a success and why
- whether it was a failure and why.

Rosa Parkes being fingerprinted after breaking the bus segregation laws, 1955.

Key words

Boycott A group action which shows disapproval for certain conditions imposed on that group.

1955: The Montgomery bus boycott

On the evening of 1 December 1955, Rosa Parkes caught a bus in the town of Montgomery, Alabama, where the segregation laws were strict. When Rosa refused to give up her seat to a white man, she was arrested and jailed.

In response to Rosa's arrest, a meeting was held the next evening where it was decided to **boycott** the buses. Thousands of leaflets were sent all over the city persuading black people to join the boycott.

As black people were the main bus users, most of the buses on the first day of the boycott were very empty. The boycott eventually ended eleven months later on 13 November 1956, when the Supreme Court declared that segregation on buses was illegal.

SOURCE E

Elizabeth Eckford is jeered by a white crowd as she tries to enter the Central High School at Little Rock, September 1957.

1957: Resistance at Little Rock

In September 1957 the town of Little Rock, Arkansas, decided to admit nine talented black students to the all-white Central High School. This was its first step towards the **integration** of black and white students. However, white people protested and the Govenor of Arkansas sent the Arkansas National Guard to prevent the black students from entering the school.

In response, President Eisenhower sent 1000 paratroopers to Little Rock on 24 September. They escorted the black students to their lessons. This did not stop the white students' abuse, however. Insults were hurled at the black students, their lockers were destroyed and one student even had acid sprayed in her face. Despite this, in May 1958 Ernest Green became the first black graduate of Central High School.

Key words

Integration The mixing of peoples of different races who had previously been segregated.

1960: Greensboro sit-in

On 1 February 1960 four black students sat down and demanded service at an all-white lunch counter at a Woolworth store in Greensboro, North Carolina. When the store closed that evening, they had still not been served. The next day, a larger group of students returned and the same thing happened.

Similar protests soon followed in other departments stores across the south. Black students would sit patiently at the lunch counters of stores waiting to be served. If they were served, they moved on to the next lunch counter. If they were not, they would not move until they were served. If they were arrested, a new group of students would take their place. Many of these sit-ins, as the demonstrations were known, were attacked and nearly 3600 protesters were arrested. In spite of the provocation, the students always followed a policy of non-violence.

White Americans pick on civil rights demonstrators holding a sit-in in a sandwich bar, 1960.

As part of the sit-in campaign, many black people in the north boycotted department stores and many white customers stayed away from the stores, fearing violence. Store owners, frightened that they would lose trade, eventually opened their lunch counters to black people.

1963: protest in Alabama

In April 1963 civil rights leaders organised a campaign of marches and sit-ins against segregation in Birmingham, Alabama. More than 30,000 people took part.

On 2 May 1963 a large group of black children marched towards the white area of town to protest against segregation. The following day, more children marched. Birmingham's Chief of Police, Bull Connor, ordered the police to use water cannons on the crowd. Police dogs were also set on the marchers.

After three days of protest, more than 2000 people, mostly children, had been arrested and imprisoned. The actions of Bull Connor shocked many Americans who saw the scenes on their television sets. President Kennedy demanded that segregation should be ended in Birmingham. A week later, the council in Birmingham gave into the protesters' demands.

FROM SLAVERY TO CIVIL RIGHTS.

1964: the Civil Rights Act

On 2 July 1964 the Civil Rights Act was passed.

- Segregation in public places was banned.
- Racial discrimination was banned in employment.
- An Equal Employment Opportunities Commission was established to investigate complaints of discrimination.

In 1965 the Voting Rights Act was passed to end racial discrimination over the right to vote.

How much had been achieved by the end of the 1960s?

Despite the changes to the law, black Americans continued to live in the more deprived areas, such as ghettos, with poor housing and inadequate services like schools. Unemployment among black people was high and white people earned higher wages than black people.

Black people continued to face racist attacks from white people. They were often the victims of police harassment and, in some cases, brutality.

TASKS...

In small groups, design and produce a board game for year 8 or 9 pupils to help them learn about the Civil Rights Movement in the USA in the 1950s and 1960s. Use the following advice to help you. **WS**

- You will have to think carefully about the design of your board game. You might want to include some of the most important events in the design of the board itself.
- Your board game must contain threat and opportunity cards, as these will be the 'educational' parts of the game. Threat cards will contain information about the failures of the Civil Rights movement and these should penalise the player who gets them. Opportunity cards will contain information about the successes of the Civil Rights movement and these should reward the player who gets them.
- Produce a set of rules for your game. Make sure they are clear and easy to follow.

When you have completed your game, play another group's game. Evaluate it by explaining what its strengths were and how it could be improved.

What part did Martin Luther King play in the Civil Rights Movement?

In the 1950s and 1960s the Civil Rights Movement was driven by a number of influential civil rights leaders. Of these leaders, Martin Luther King was one of the most prominent.

Martin Luther King was born in Atlanta on 15 January 1929. He graduated with a degree in sociology in 1948 and was awarded a doctoral degree in theology in 1955. In 1954 he became pastor of a Baptist Church in Montgomery. He was also a prominent member of the National Association for the Advancement of Coloured People (NAACP), an organisation dedicated to campaigning for the civil rights of black Americans.

The Montgomery bus boycott

On page 103 you read how an incident with Rosa Parks sparked a boycott of travelling on buses. King played a key role in organising the boycott. During the boycott he was arrested and his home was bombed. King responded to this treatment with the words on the right.

We believe in law and order. We do not support violence. We want to love our enemies. If I am stopped, our work will not stop, for what we are doing is right.

*Hate **begets** hate; violence begets violence; toughness begets greater toughness. We must meet the forces of hate with the power of love. Our aim must never be to defeat or humiliate the white man, but to win his friendship and understanding.*

The Southern Christian Leadership Conference

In 1957 Martin Luther King was elected President of the Southern Christian Leadership Conference (SCLC). In the next eleven years, King delivered more than 2000 speeches in different places across the USA. He spoke wherever there was injustice, protest and action. He also wrote five books and several articles.

Key words

Beget To produce an effect.

'I have a dream ...'

On 28 August 1963 some 250,000 people marched on Washington. Martin Luther King delivered his famous 'I have a dream' speech to

protestors who had gathered at the Lincoln Memorial in Washington DC. His speech expressed the hopes of the Civil Rights Movement.

Martin Luther King waves to marchers as they gather at the Lincoln Memorial in Washington, 28 August 1963.

In his speech King said:

> I have a dream that my four little children will one day live in a nation where they will not be judged by the colour of their skin, but by the content of their character. From every mountainside, let freedom ring, and speed up that day when all of God's children, black men and white men, Jews and Gentiles, Protestants and Catholics, will be able to join hands and sing in the words of the old **Negro spiritual**, 'Free at last! Free at last! Thank God Almighty, we are free at last!'

Key words

Negro spiritual A black American religious song.

The march on Washington was a great success. The approach adopted by King and the SCLC helped lead to the Civil Rights Act of 1964, which banned segregation in public buildings as well as discrimination in education, housing and employment.

Martin Luther King is awarded the Nobel Peace Prize

In 1964 Martin Luther King became the youngest man to be awarded the Nobel Peace Prize. He gave the prize money to the Civil Rights Movement.

The Voting Rights Campaign, 1965

In April 1965 King lead 25,000 protestors from Selma to Montgomery, the capital of Alabama. Within a few months of the march, the Voting Rights Act became law in August 1965.

> We must have our freedom now. We must have the right to vote. We must have equal protection of the law.

Opposition to King

Martin Luther King did not win the support of all black Americans. In 1960, following sit-in protests at lunch counters (see pages 104–5), the Student Non-violent Coordinating Committee (SNCC) was formed. This organisation criticised King's leadership style. King was also criticised by young activists for his decision not to participate in certain protests.

Some black leaders challenged whether King's non-violent methods were effective. Malcolm X was the spokesman for the Nation of Islam. He believed in the use of violence to defeat white rule (see the speech bubble below). Stokely Carmichael, who spoke of 'Black Power' in 1966, was also openly critical of King's leadership and methods.

Don't try to be friends with somebody who's depriving you of your rights. They are not your friends. They're your enemies. Treat them like that. Fight and you'll get your freedom.

Assassination

In the spring of 1968 Martin Luther King travelled to Memphis, Tennessee, to support black sanitation workers who were on strike. In Memphis, he gave what was to be his final speech.

Key words

Legacy What a person leaves behind after their death. A legacy can be physical, such as gifts, or it can be the influence of their ideas on future generations.

The next day, on 4 April, King was assassinated by James Earl Ray while standing on the balcony of his motel room. Following his death, riots took place in more than 100 cities in the USA.

Martin Luther King's **legacy** lives on today in the USA. His birthday is a national holiday and the hotel where he was shot is now the National Civil Rights Museum.

TASKS...

1 What were the key factors that made Martin Luther King a success as a civil rights leader?

2 Why was Martin Luther King's leadership criticised by some younger black Americans?

3 Get into groups of six. Imagine you have been asked to make a TV documentary looking back at the life of Martin Luther King and explaining whether he made a positive contribution to the Civil Rights Movement. Use the guidelines below to help you plan and write your documentary.

Decide what your documentary will show. Will it support the work of Martin Luther King, or will it be critical?

Your documentary should include:

- an overview of the key events in the life of Martin Luther King
- an interview with Martin Luther King explaining his key beliefs and his view of events
- interviews with leading figures such as Rosa Parks, who explain why Martin Luther King is so important in their lives
- interviews with opponents who will question the impact Martin Luther King had on events
- a conclusion in which you evaluate the importance of Martin Luther King in the history of the Civil Rights Movement in the USA, both in his own lifetime and in the longer term.

Use a larger copy of this planning sheet to help you plan and write your documentary.

Scene: Explain who will be in the shot/what the shot will show:	Long shot
	Close up
	Other
Commentary/script:	

4 Present your ideas to the rest of the class. Evaluate each other's presentations and give them a mark out of 15.

- Award up to 5 marks for the quality of the biographical details included.
- Award up to 5 marks for how well the work of Martin Luther King has been covered.
- Award up to 5 marks for how well his importance has been explained.

Add a comment to explain your decisions.

Key words

Epitaph A brief statement summarising the life of somebody who has died.

Plenary

If you had to write an **epitaph** of no more than 20 words to go on the tombstone of Martin Luther King, what would it be? Share your ideas with the rest of the class.

HOW 'GREAT' WAS THE BRITISH EMPIRE?

DID EVERYONE BENEFIT FROM THE 'GREAT' BRITISH EMPIRE?

Objectives

In this section you will find out:
- why Britain wanted an empire in the nineteenth century
- whether everyone benefited from being part of the British Empire.

To investigate these ideas you will:
- select and organise source evidence on mind maps
- use the sources to write from a specific viewpoint.

Starter

Look at Source A, which was a popular image of its time. Now look at Source B, which shows what a member of the British government thought about the empire.

In June every year, British people celebrated 'Empire Day'. This photo is from an Empire Day celebration in 1922.

We are the British, engaged in the magnificent work of governing an inferior race.

Lord Mayo, Viceroy (governor) of India, 1869–72.

💡 *What words would you use to describe the British Empire as it appears in Source A?*

💡 *In what ways does Source B support Source A?*

💡 *Can you think of anybody who might object to the Lord Mayo's words? Give reasons for your answer.*

What was the British Empire?

When one country gains control and has power over other countries, it is said to have an empire. The countries that make up an empire are called colonies. Throughout the nineteenth century and the first half of the twentieth century, Britain had the biggest empire in the world. This empire covered about one-quarter of the world's land surface.

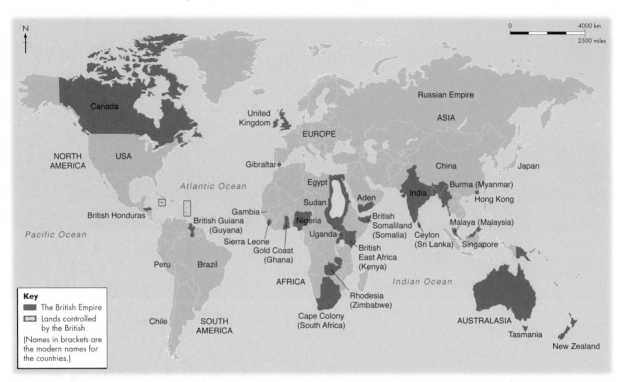

A map of the British Empire in 1900.

What benefits do you think the empire would bring to the people of Britain?

The benefits of the British Empire

The young boy woke up and got out of bed.
He pulled on his trousers and, as it was cold, his woolly jumper. He went downstairs and made himself a cup of tea and a bowl of Shredded Wheat for breakfast. Then he put on his rubber-soled shoes and went to school. After a long hard day, he came home. His mum had made lamb curry for dinner – his favourite. At the end of the evening, the boy had a mug of hot cocoa before going to bed.

This young boy's day is similar to that of many other people living in Britain. You probably eat and wear some of the things that he does. Many of the things we use everyday originally came from countries in the British Empire.

💡 Look at the boy's day again. For each of the products underlined, try to work out which colony it came from. Use the map on page 112 to help you.

Use the map on page 112 to help you.

Access to cheap **raw materials** was one of the reasons why Britain benefited from having a large empire.

💡 What other benefits or reasons can you think of why countries like Britain wanted an empire? Work with a partner to brainstorm your ideas, then share them with the class.

Why did the British Empire grow between 1750 and 1900?

There were several reasons why Britain increased the size of its empire between 1750 and 1900.

- By 1900 British merchants were importing goods from all over the world. Initially, companies like the British East India Company had been set up to control the trading posts in these countries. Gradually, the British government became involved until it ran the countries. Now trade, and the sea routes to and from the countries, could be closely controlled.

- Many British people were in favour of the empire getting bigger so that Christian **missionaries** could 'civilise' the native people and convert them to Christianity.

- Some people, keen for adventure, took the role of missionaries and 'discovered' new countries. Explorers like Captain Cook were competing with other explorers to be the first to 'discover' new lands, and many people in Britain were interested in following their adventures.

A map of the countries which controlled Africa by 1900.

- European countries competed with each other to gain the biggest empire, for example different European countries fought to gain control of Africa in what became known as the 'Scramble for Africa'. By 1900 European countries controlled 90 per cent of Africa, which was 80 per cent more than they had controlled just 30 years earlier in 1870.

- As well as providing land and raw materials, colonies could also provide people to work cheaply and, if necessary, fight for the country that controlled them.

SOURCE C

Men sometimes died fighting for the country that controlled them. These headstones are from a New Zealand First World War graveyard.

TASKS...

1 Copy and complete the mind map below. Add details around each big reason to show why you think Britain would have benefited from having an empire.

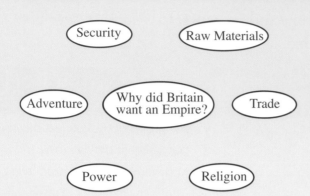

2 a) For each detail you have entered on your mind map, write down what effect you think this might have had on the native people of the colonies.

b) Are your effects negative or positive? Mark them with a +(plus) or –(minus) symbol.

c) Compare your effects with a partner and discuss any differences.

Did everyone benefit from the British Empire?

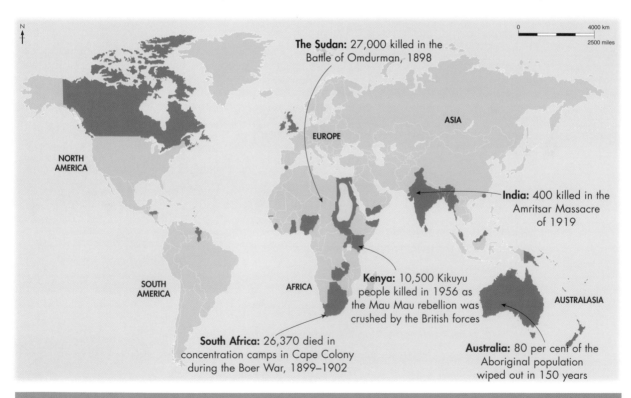

The Sudan: 27,000 killed in the Battle of Omdurman, 1898

India: 400 killed in the Amritsar Massacre of 1919

Kenya: 10,500 Kikuyu people killed in 1956 as the Mau Mau rebellion was crushed by the British forces

South Africa: 26,370 died in concentration camps in Cape Colony during the Boer War, 1899–1902

Australia: 80 per cent of the Aboriginal population wiped out in 150 years

A map showing what Britain did to some of its colonies.

What do you think the map tells us about the British Empire? How is this different from what has been suggested so far about the empire?

It is clear from the map on page 115 that not everyone benefited from the British Empire. Most often, it was the native people living in the British colonies who benefited least and actually suffered under British rule. The map below and Sources D to G suggest several reasons why they suffered.

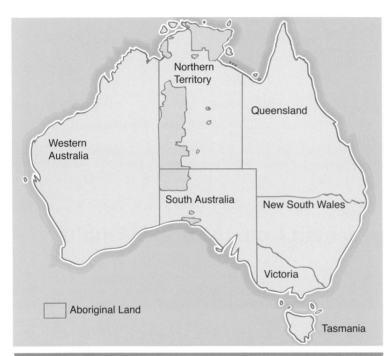

The land Australian Aborigines were allowed to live on. British settlers were also known to hunt Aborigines for sport.

The profits of the colonies did not go to benefit the native people, who were desperately poor and whose cheap labour allowed the big profits to be made. Instead, they went to wealthy shareholders in London.

From a modern history book.

I will lay down my policy on this native question. Either you will receive the natives on an equal footing as citizens or call them a subject race. I have made up my mind. The native is to be treated as a child and denied the vote.

Said by Cecil Rhodes, Prime Minister of Cape Colony (South Africa), in 1894.

Can these thieves really be our rulers? These thieves import a huge number of goods, made in their own country, and sell them in our markets, stealing our wealth and taking life from our people. Can those who steal the harvest from our fields and doom us to hunger, fever and plague really be our rulers? Can foreigners really be our rulers, foreigners who impose on us ever more taxes?

Leaflet written in Bengal, 1907.

British customs were sometimes forced on the native peoples, and local customs, culture and religions were ignored.

From a modern history book.

TASKS...

Look at the map on page 116 and Sources D to G. Each one suggests a different reason why native people did not benefit from British rule.

1 Copy and complete the mind map to show these reasons. One question you need to think about has already been written on the mind map. Try to think of the other reasons yourself – one for each source. Add them to the mind map with details to explain each reason. If two or more of your reasons link together, draw these links on your mind map and explain each link.

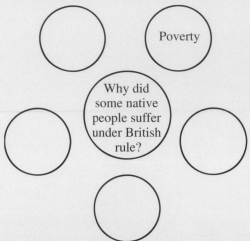

Poverty

Why did some native people suffer under British rule?

2 Compare your mind map with a partner's. Have you come up with the same reasons? Discuss any differences in your mind maps. Do you think you need to change yours in any way?

Plenary

Look at Source H, then answer the questions that follow.

SOURCE H

Law and order is perhaps the most important advantage that we British gave to our colonies. We took the ideas of liberty, equality, justice and democracy to the colonies. With these came the advantages of civilisation, closely followed by the benefits of technology.

What were these advantages? First – ease of travel; second – education; third – public health. In addition to the fight against disease, our experts helped to provide sanitation and pure water supplies. There were also improvements in agriculture.

A British official writing in the twentieth century.

💡 How do you think Source H is different from the other evidence you have seen in this section?

💡 Why do you think Source H tells a different story? Think about who wrote it and why.

Re-write Source H from a native person's viewpoint using evidence from this chapter to support the view.

HOW SUCCESSFULLY DID LOCAL PEOPLE RESIST BRITISH RULE?

Objectives

In this section you will find out how:

- how people living in India were affected by British rule
- how successfully Indians resisted British rule.

To investigate these ideas you will:

- look at methods of protest and resistance against the British in India
- look at both sides of an argument
- take part in a debate or discussion.

Starter

Take a look at Source A.

The Indian leader, Mohandas Gandhi, and the politician, feminist and poet, Sarojini Naidu, leading the 'March to the Sea' in 1930.

💡 *What do you think might be happening in this picture?*

💡 *Try to think of three questions you would like to ask about this picture so that you can find out more.*

TIMELINE
British rule in India, 1756–1947

1756   Black Hole of Calcutta: the Nawab of Bengal attacks a British settlement in Calcutta and imprisons 146 colonists in a space measuring 6 metres by 8 metres, causing 123 of them to die.

1757   The Battle of Plassey: Robert Clive leads his troops to victory against the Nawab of Bengal. This earns Clive the title 'The Father of India'.
The British East India Company increase their control of Indian trade.

1833   An education system is introduced to teach the English language to Indian children.

1857   The Indian Mutiny: there is a violent rebellion against British involvement in India. As part of the rebellion, Indians massacre the families of British troops – 200 women and children are killed (see Source B).

1858   The British government takes over the running and control of India from the British East India Company.

1861   Indians are allowed to hold positions on councils in the provinces (states) and to become magistrates (supervise legal decisions).

British officers and their wives are shown being massacred during the Indian Mutiny. From a book published in 1858.

1877   Queen Victoria is given the title 'Empress of India'. A British leader, known as Viceroy, is put in charge of governing India.

1885   The first meeting of the Indian National Congress, an organisation to represent the political ideas of Indian people.

1906   The Muslim League is set up to protect Muslim interests. (Muslims make up about one-quarter of the population; most of the rest are Hindus.)

1909   The Indian Councils Act increases Indian representation in government but has no real power.

1914 India is automatically involved in the First World War because it is part of the British Empire. Indian soldiers are sent to fight in the trenches in France and Belgium (see Source C).

1919 13 April, the Amritsar Massacre: a peaceful protest against British rule is broken up by British soldiers, resulting in the deaths of 400 people. There is a national outcry. In response, the British pass the Government of India Act, which divides power between British and Indian representatives. However, only 5 million wealthy Indians (2.8 per cent of the population) are given the vote. The Indian National Congress refuses to accept the Act.

1920 Mohandas Gandhi, who believes in peaceful and non-violent protest, becomes leader of the Indian National Congress. He organises a large peaceful campaign against the British.

1930 Gandhi leads a peaceful campaign called the Salt March.

1935 The Second Government of India Act sets up elected parliaments in eleven provinces. All Indians are given the vote, but Britain continues to have overall control. The Indian National Congress refuses to co-operate.

1939 The Second World War begins. The British viceroy declares that India is at war against Germany, against the wishes of the Indian National Congress.

1947 15 August: India becomes independent.

SOURCE C

A photograph of Indian troops in France during the First World War.

SOURCE D

Independence Day celebrations in India, 15 August 1947.

In the pages that follow (121–4), you will look at two events from the timeline to compare their successes and failures.

The Indian Mutiny, 1857

British influence in India began mainly because of the British East India Company and its desire to look after its trading interests in the area. The company set up its own army. It recruited Indian troops and put British officers in charge of them. In fact, 96 per cent of the 300,000-strong British army in India were Indians.

However, many Indians were uneasy about British control – especially when Christian missionaries started to spread Christianity into the continent. This unease came to a head in 1857 when the British government introduced a new type of rifle into the Indian army. The Indian soldiers were told to grease the cartridge of the rifle with cow and pig fat. This was extremely offensive to **Hindus** and **Muslims**. To Hindus, the cow is sacred, and Muslims do not use or eat any products made from pig.

Key words

Hindus Followers of the Hindu religion.

Muslims Followers of Islam.

The British realised their mistake and replaced the animal fats with vegetable oils. But the damage had already been done. In May 1857, an Indian soldier shot his British officer and the violence quickly spread.

This mutiny was a serious threat to British power in India and an opportunity to gain freedom from British influence.

TASKS...

1 Imagine you are a member of the British government. Remember that at this time it was the East India Company which controlled how India was run. How do you think the government should react to the Indian mutiny?

Mind map some possible solutions and decide on the best one. Share your ideas with the person next to you.

How successful was the Indian Mutiny?

It is clear from the timeline on pages 119–20 that the Indian Mutiny did not force the British out of India. But does this mean that it was a complete failure?

The Indian Mutiny was a waste of time. Indians lost their lives in the violence and the result was an increase in British control, not less. The mutiny shattered any hope of India becoming independent.

We showed the British that they could not ignore our beliefs and get away with it. If they want to stay in India, they must show some respect for our beliefs.

TASKS...

1 The statements in the speech bubbles represent the two sides of the argument about the results of the Indian Mutiny. Which side do you think is closest to the truth? Why?

2 Look at statements **a–j** showing the results of the Indian Mutiny. Decide in pairs which viewpoint, the view of the British or of the mutineers, each statement supports. **WS**

a) The mutiny did not spread throughout the country.

b) **Sikh** soldiers remained loyal to the British. The Sikh army was strong and well-trained.

c) The mutiny made the British more defensive about their empire.

d) Bahadur Shah, the leader of the rebellion, was a poor leader and general.

e) To regain control the British used violence against, and massacred, innocent people – including women and children.

f) British authority collapsed in some areas.

g) The mutiny created bitterness between Indians and their rulers.

h) The mutiny brought about some changes, for example greater acceptance of the different religions in India. Indians began to be allowed to hold positions in the Civil Service.

i) The Indian rebels committed violent atrocities towards the British.

j) As a result of the mutiny, in 1858 Britain abolished the East India Company and took full control of India.

3 Once you have sorted these statements, you should reach a final judgement on how successful the Indian Mutiny was. Weigh up the evidence on each side and write a conclusion, saying which viewpoint you support and why.

Key words

Sikhs Followers of Sikhism.

The Salt March, 1930

By 1930 many Indians were beginning to demand independence from British rule and wanted to drive the British out of India. The leader of the campaign for Indian independence was Mohandas Gandhi. He was sometimes known by his people as 'Mahatma', which means 'Great Soul'.

Gandhi was a devout Hindu. Hindus are opposed to violence and killing. So Gandhi tried to achieve independence by using the non-violent method of **passive resistance**. The most famous example of this kind of resistance to British rule was the Salt March, which took place in 1930.

> ## Key words
>
> **Passive resistance** Non-violent protest, e.g. peaceful demonstrations or non-cooperation with the law.

The British had made a law forbidding Indians from making their own salt. Instead, they had to buy it from British companies at a much higher price with extra tax added on. In March 1930 Gandhi began a 200-mile march to the sea. He was joined by thousands of followers along the way. When he got there he simply bent down and picked up a chunk of sea salt from the shore.

💡 In picking up the salt, what do you think Gandhi had done?

TASKS...

1   Imagine you are a member of the British government. How would you advise all the other members to react to Gandhi's actions? Brainstorm some possible solutions and choose the one you think is best. Share your ideas with the person next to you.

How successful was the Salt March?

The Salt March was a great success. It proved that ordinary Indians could bring about change in a non-violent way. The British did not know how to deal with these tactics and were forced to listen.

Peaceful Indians died or were sent to jail as a result of this 'non-violence'. It failed to drive the British out of India.

TASKS...

1 The statements in the speech bubbles on page 123 represent the two sides of the argument about the results of the Salt March. Which side do you think is closest to the truth?

2 Statements **a–j** show the results of the Salt March. Read each statement and decide in pairs which viewpoint, that of the protestors or that of the British, each statement supports. **WS**

a) The protesters were peaceful and proved that passive resistance could result in change.

b) The protest encouraged other ordinary Indians to follow Gandhi's example and break the salt laws leading to 100,000 arrests.

c) The British reacted violently, with police beating up unarmed protesters. This wore down resistance in some areas.

d) Large sections of the salt laws were lifted because the British could not keep putting people in jail.

e) The British were not driven out of India – they remained in control.

f) Large communities of Indians did not join in the protest.

g) The violent British reaction against a peaceful protest made them look bad. They could no longer argue that the Indians were happy for the British to be in India.

h) Gandhi's non-violent protest sparked off violent Indian riots in some places.

i) Britain agreed to negotiate with Gandhi and the Indian National Congress for the first time as equals.

j) The Salt March brought worldwide publicity and new supporters to India's campaign for independence.

3 Once you have sorted the statements, you should reach a final judgement on how successful the Salt March was. Weigh up the evidence on each side and write a conclusion, saying which viewpoint you support and why.

Plenary

SOURCE E

England can hold India only by consent. We can't rule it by the sword.

Sir Charles Innes, a provincial Governor of India.

Do you agree with this statement? Use evidence from this section to support your answer and then discuss it as a class.

HOW DID LIFE CHANGE FOR JEWS LIVING IN EUROPE, 1919–45?

7

The Holocaust

6 million The number of Jews who died.

3 months The average life expectancy in **Auschwitz**.

5000 The number of homosexuals who died.

200,000 The number of gypsies who died.

126385 The number tattooed on someone's arm.

300 The number of calories a day people were fed in the Warsaw Ghetto.

3 to 15 minutes The time it took kill 1000 people in a gas chamber at Auschwitz.

2000 The number of people cremated at Auschwitz every day.

38,000 The number of pairs of men's shoes found at Auschwitz.

836,255 The number of women's dresses found at Auschwitz.

2 minutes, 2 seconds The time it took to die from a lethal injection.

170,000 The number of people murdered in a **euthanasia** programme.

18,000 The number of Jewish children sent to safety in Britain.

10,000 The number of unburied bodies found by British troops in the Bergen-Belsen concentration camp.

78,000 The number of Jews who left Germany in the first three years of Nazi rule.

28 The number of known groups of Jewish resistance fighters.

22 The number of concentration camps in Europe.

22 to 29 kilograms What most women weighed after Auschwitz was liberated.

7 tonnes The weight of unsold hair found when Auschwitz was liberated.

90 x 90 centimetres The size of a punishment room in which four prisoners were expected to stand.

Key words

Auschwitz The largest Nazi concentration camp, Auschwitz-Birkenau in Poland.

Euthanasia Prematurally ending someone's life.

💡 What are your first thoughts after reading these statements?

💡 Which figure alarms you most? Why?

💡 What do you think is the problem with using numbers and statements to find out about an event?

💡 What five questions would you ask to find out more about the Holocaust?

HOW DID THE EXPERIENCES OF JEWS LIVING IN GERMANY CHANGE BETWEEN 1919 AND 1945?

Objectives

In this section you will find out:
- how Jewish people's experiences changed in Germany between 1919 and 1945
- the different steps that Adolf Hitler took to influence people's attitudes and feelings towards the Jews.

To investigate these ideas you will:
- make a comparison of sources
- create a mind map to show the changes over a period of time.

Starter

Read Sources A and B.

Then answer the questions on page 127.

SOURCE **A**

Jews and Germans killed during the First World War were buried side by side. This graveyard is in Germany.

SOURCE **B**

A poster published in 1920 which explains that over 12,000 German Jews were killed fighting for their country in the First World War. The poster is addressed to 'All German mothers'.

💡 *What do you think Sources A and B have in common?*

💡 *Is there any evidence to suggest that Jews were generally accepted in Germany after the First World War?*

Why did German people begin to dislike Jews after 1919?

Key words

Anti-Semitic Against Jews and their belief.

There were many Jews living in Germany at the time of the First World War and they were well integrated into the social, political and economic aspects of German life. However, some Germans had always expressed **anti-Semitic** views.

After Germany lost the First World War, it was forced to sign the humiliating Treaty of Versailles in 1919. The Treaty said that Germany was to blame for the war and that it should therefore pay for the damage the war had caused. This was a vast amount of money, and would be difficult to pay as Germany had lost important industrial and agricultural areas in the Treaty.

The German people were angry. Some Germans looked for people they could blame for their country's problems, such as politicians, foreign countries, or the Jews. The Jews did well in business and became quite wealthy after the First World War. Some Germans didn't like this and accused the Jews of using Germany's misfortune to their own advantage.

How did Hitler influence what the German people thought about Jews?

In the 1920s Adolf Hitler became leader of a small and extreme political party (later called the Nazi Party). He began to openly criticise and blame the Jews for causing Germany's problems.

After becoming Chancellor of Germany in 1933, Hitler quickly seized control. By the mid 1930s he controlled the media, the armed forces, education, the economy, leisure time and the culture of the German people.

Hitler believed that some races and individuals were superior to others. He saw the Jews as the lowest of the 'inferior races' and referred to them as 'race polluters'. Hitler thought that German people were the 'master race'. He stated that 'pure' Germans, or Aryans, should control those he saw as inferior. Hitler therefore decided to influence the minds and actions of the German people, so that they would think badly of Jews.

SOURCE C

Is there any shady undertaking, any form of foulness, in which Jews do not participate?
… The Jews want to corrupt the white race which they hate … the black-haired Jewish youth waits for hours on end, glaring like a devil and spying on the unsuspicious German girl whom he plans to seduce, corrupting her and removing her from the bosom of her own people.

Hitler's anti-Semitic views from *Mein Kampf*, written in 1924.

In Source C, what words does Hitler use to portray Jews in a negative way and Germans in a positive way?

MEMO FROM HITLER

1 Close down anti-Nazi newspapers and only print news that favours the viewpoint of the Nazis.
2 Give all German children lessons on how to be proud Aryans and always tell them they are better than Jews.
3 Introduce laws that forbid Jews from marrying Germans and stop them from being German citizens.
4 Do not let Jews work for the government or have any other important jobs.
5 Let people destroy and vandalise any shops owned by Jews.
6 Burn all books that Jews have written.
7 Show anti-Semitic films at the cinemas.
8 Let teachers pick on Jewish children in class and allow them to be laughed at by other children.
9 All Jews must leave the armed forces.
10 Jews are not allowed to trade or own businesses.
11 All Jewish artwork must be destroyed.
12 Jews are no longer allowed to go to university.
13 The army and the police have the power to arrest and interrogate Jews without having to give a reason.
14 All German children must join a Nazi Youth group, in which they will be taught about Nazi beliefs.
15 Make cheap radios, then put them in public places so that everyone can listen to Nazi speeches.
16 Only books that favour Nazi beliefs are allowed to be published and sold.

The Jews are aliens in Germany. In 1933 there were 66,060,000 inhabitants of the German Reich, of whom 499, 862 were Jews. What is the percentage of aliens in Germany?

An exercise from a German textbook, 1933

German children being examined for suitable Aryan characteristics. Hitler described 'pure' Aryans as healthy and physically strong, with blond hair and blue eyes.

A cartoon from the front page of a German newspaper in 1935. The cartoon shows a Jewish butcher and his wife making sausages from rats.

💡 What messages do these sources give about Jews?

HOW DID LIFE CHANGE FOR JEWS LIVING IN EUROPE, 1919–45?

TASKS...

1 a) Copy and complete the chart below using 'Hitler's memo' and Sources C to F.

Give examples to show how Hitler used his power to make life difficult for the Jews.

Area of life which Hitler influenced	How Hitler used his influence to change Jews' lives	How might this change German people's thoughts and actions?
Media		
Education		
Armed forces		
Culture		
Economy		
Leisure time		

b) Look at what you have written in the third column on your chart. Using two different coloured highlighter pens, mark all the things that you think were:

- difficult for the Jews (one colour)
- unbearable for the Jews (another colour).

Don't forget to make a note of your colour code on the chart.

2 How difficult do you think life became for Jews after Hitler began to control the German people's minds and actions?

3 Create a mind map to show how the experiences of Jews changed when Hitler came to power.

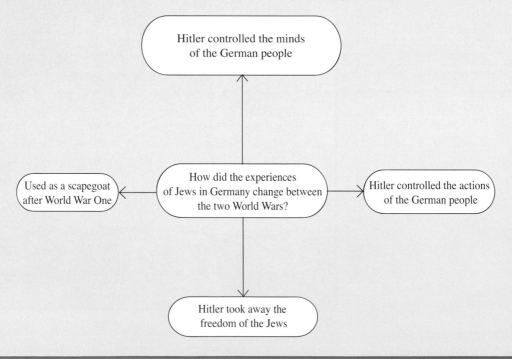

How did Hitler take away the Jews' freedom?

Between 1933 and 1939 Hitler introduced several laws that made life very difficult for Jews living in Germany (see the timeline below). The first laws passed aimed to segregate Germany's 500,000 Jews from the rest of the population. Other laws took away their freedoms and damaged any respect they once had.

TIMELINE
Anti-Semitism in Germany, 1933–9

1933
- 30 January: Hitler becomes Chancellor of Germany.
- 1 April: A boycott of Jewish shops is carried out.
- 7 April: Jews are banned from working in public services.
- 26 April: The SS (Hitler's bodyguard) are given the power to arrest and question whoever they want.
- 10 May: 20,000 books are burned, many are by Jewish authors.

1934
- 5 March: Jewish actors are banned from appearing on stage and screen.
- 7 June: Jewish companies are no longer mentioned on the radio.
- 22 July: Jewish students can no longer sit law exams.
- 1 October: Jewish newspapers are no longer sold or displayed in public.

1935
- May: Jews are forbidden from serving in the armed services and are banned from going to some public places.
- 15 September: Nuremberg Laws removed Jews' rights as German citizens. Marriage between Jews and non-Jews banned.

1936
- The Olympic Games are held in Berlin. Anti-Semitic actions are 'stopped'.

1937
- 26 April: Jews have to register all their possessions.
- 23 July: Jews have to carry identity cards.
- 17 August: Jews' names are changed. 'Israel' is added to a man's name and 'Sara' to a woman's.
- 28 October: Polish Jews are deported to ghettos and labour camps.

1938
- 9– 10 October: *Kristallnacht* (Night of Broken Glass) – a night of violence against the Jews.
- 12 November: Jews can no longer own shops.
- 16 November: All Jews are dismissed from German schools.
- 3 December: Jews are banned from entering cinemas and theatres.

1939
- Jewish doctors lose their qualifications and all Jews lose their jobs.
- 12 October: Jews are deported from Austria to Poland.
- 28 October: Jews in Poland have to wear a yellow star.

TASKS...

1 Return to your mind map. Use the timeline on page 131 to add extra information to show how Jews in Germany lost rights and freedom after 1933.

  Are any of the changes to Jews' lives linked? If so, draw a line between them and explain how they are linked.

2 What do you think was the main factor influencing the change in Jewish experiences in Germany between 1919 and 1939? Justify your answer.

Plenary

Look at the following three statements.

a) The Jews were used as **scapegoats** and blamed for Germany's defeat after the First World War.

b) Hitler used his control over the German people to influence their minds and actions.

c) Jews' lives only began to change when their respect and freedom was removed

Which of the three statements do you most agree with? Why?

Now write a fourth statement of no more than fifteen words that explains the main factor that led to the changes in the lives of Jews in Germany between 1919 and 1939.

Key words

Scapegoat Someone who is blamed for other people's problems.

WHAT WAS LIFE LIKE FOR JEWS LIVING IN THE WARSAW GHETTO BETWEEN 1939 AND 1945?

Objectives

In this section you will find out:
- how Jewish people's experiences changed in Europe between 1939 and 1945
- how Jewish people throughout Europe reacted to the changes in their circumstances
- what life was like for Jews living in the Warsaw Ghetto.

To investigate these ideas you will:
- discuss the options available to some Jews
- complete a diary to reveal what life was like in the Warsaw Ghetto.

Starter

Look at the cartoon below, which shows a Jewish man considering the options available to his family in 1939.

> *We could take the few important things we need and go into hiding at some point next week. We must act quickly if we are going to do this.*

> *We could pack up all our things, sell everything and just leave Germany.*

> *We could ignore everything that is going on around us. The Nazis are not going to hurt us. I fought for Germany in the First World War. Surely it can't be that hard to stay and wait for things to calm down?*

With a partner, discuss the advantages and disadvantages of each option given in the cartoon.

- 💡 *What other questions would you like to ask about each option?*
- 💡 *Which option would you take? Why?*
- 💡 *What further problems would you have to take into account?*

The Warsaw Ghetto

By the early 1940s Hitler had conquered a large part of Europe and was beginning to put into place his aim of increasing the *Lebensraum* (living space) for the Aryans. In order to segregate the Jewish population and also to provide more living space for Aryans across Europe, Jews were rounded up by the Nazis, especially in Germany and Poland. They were forced to leave their homes and possessions, and to live in ghettos. These ghettos were walled-off areas that separated the Jews from the rest of the population of the town or city. The best-known ghetto was the Warsaw Ghetto, in Poland, where more than 400,000 Jews (one-third of the city's total population) were forced to live in an area that was only 2 per cent of the total size of Warsaw.

The conditions in the ghettos were extremely harsh, with overcrowded living quarters, poor hygiene and little food. Between ten and twenty people would have lived in one room, often without sanitation, water or fuel. Diseases such as **typhus** spread very quickly, killing thousands. More than 2000 people living in the ghettos died from starvation each month.

Key words

Typhus A dangerous illness spread by lice.

SOURCE A

SOURCE B

The closed ghetto cut the Jews off completely from the rest of the world. It prevented Jews from making contact with non-Jews, and left them isolated, insulated and in a state of choking congestion.

Written by Israel Gutman, who lived in the Warsaw Ghetto.

A photograph showing living conditions in the Warsaw Ghetto, 1939.

SOURCE C

On the streets children are crying in vain, children who are dying of hunger. They howl, beg, sing, moan and shiver with cold. Without underwear, without clothing, without shoes, in rags, sacks, flannel, which are bound in strips around their wasting skeletons. Already completely grown up at the age of five, gloomy and weary of life. Every day and every night, hundreds of these children die. I no longer look at the people when I hear groaning and sobbing. I cross the road.

A description of life in the Warsaw Ghetto by a visitor.

SOURCE D

Queuing for food in the Warsaw Ghetto, 1939.

SOURCE E

There are about 27,000 apartments with an average number of two and a half rooms. Occupancy therefore works out at 15.1 people per apartment and six to seven people per room.

The SS officer in charge of Warsaw Ghetto reported these details to his superior.

SOURCE F

Jewish masses, the hour is drawing near. You must be prepared to resist. Not a single Jew should go to the railroad cars. Those who are not able to put up active resistance should resist passively, go into hiding. Our slogan must be, 'All are ready to die as human beings'.

From the public manifesto of a Jewish fighting organisation in Warsaw, autumn 1942.

Key words

Deportation The transportation or expulsion of a person from a country.

Despite these harsh conditions, many Jews living in the ghettos did their best to make their lives bearable. They continued to go to lectures, to practise their religious beliefs and to observe religious holidays – even though these were forbidden. Others formed resistance groups and tried to stop the **deportations** to camps.

SOURCE G

Jews in ghettos grouped together and organised themselves to try to keep their sanity and stay alive. Some Jews worked as couriers, travelling from ghetto to ghetto to pass on information. It was dangerous work. Children often became smugglers, escaping from the ghettos to scavenge for food.

From a modern history book.

Key words

Concentration camps A prison camp for people who are segregated from society.

The ghettos were regarded by the Nazis as temporary holding places for the Jews. After rounding them up into the ghettos, the Nazis then organised transport to take them to **concentration camps** and extermination camps. Once all the Jews were finally removed, these ghettos were then 'liquidated' (destroyed).

TASKS...

You are going to write a diary account of what life was like in the Warsaw Ghetto using Sources A to G to help you make your account realistic. But before you begin your writing, you need to do some preparation.

1 a) Copy and complete the chart below to show what it was like in the Warsaw Ghetto. Use the information from this chapter and Sources A to G to provide evidence of the different aspects of life in the Warsaw Ghetto. **WS**

b) Once you have completed the chart, think carefully about each of these aspects and the evidence you have found, for example what do you think it was like eating so little food? Add a third column to the table, 'My thoughts'. In this column make a note against each aspect to help you put your thoughts into words.

Aspect of life in Warsaw Ghetto	Evidence	My thoughts
Food		
Morale		
Religion		
Housing		
Other		

2 **WS** Now write your diary account of life in the ghetto. Remember to comment on each new aspect of life and on whether life was totally unbearable at all times. Write a detailed and emotional account in the first person and present tense.

You may also carry out your own research on life in the ghetto. Include the extra information in your diary and you will be given credit for this.

Plenary

Write down three words that you think best describe life in the Warsaw Ghetto. Share these with the person next to you. Explain why you have chosen these words. How do they compare with the rest of your class?

WHY DID SO FEW PEOPLE SURVIVE THE AUSCHWITZ-BIRKENAU CONCENTRATION CAMP?

Objectives

In this section you will find out:

- how Jewish people's experiences changed in Europe between 1939 and 1945
- what life was like in the Auschwitz-Birkenau concentration camp
- why so few people survived life in the camp.

To investigate these ideas you will:

- study a poem about the camp
- look at evidence about life in the camp.

Starter

Read the poem below, which is about the Auschwitz-Birkenau concentration camp. Then answer the questions that follow.

SOURCE A

What big heavy doors!
Strange lingering odour,
faint but still here … strong disinfectant.
'Stand round the shower point.'
Wait for the water. Don't think about the crowd.
They don't notice your degradation.
They can't see your shaved head from all the rest!

My God! … They're locking those bloody great doors!
Why? It can't be!
No, the water will come in a minute.
Don't cry, just be patient,
It will be over very soon.

There's a noise – up there.
He's lifting that grate.
All eyes watching, wondering.
No sound.
What are those pellets? Dry disinfectant?
Sulphur!!?

Gas! Gas! Gas! Panic!
The screams, the clutching,
Pulling, scrambling.
The total terror of realisation.

Timeless minutes climbing and scrambling.
Families forgotten. Self-preservation.
Flesh on flesh – clutching and tearing.
Gas, screams, death … silence.

A poem by Elizabeth Wyse from *The Auschwitz Poems.*

💡 *What does the poem tell you about the concentration camp?*

💡 *What do you think you are **not** told in this poem?*

💡 *What questions would you like to ask about the poem and the concentration camp?*

Hitler's Final Solution

After the outbreak of the Second World War the Nazis changed their policy towards the Jews. They wanted to get rid of as many Jews as possible, and began to make plans for how to deal effectively with what they called the 'Jewish problem'. In 1941 they came up with a plan which was known as the Final Solution. The Jews would be dealt with in two ways: they would either be worked to death or executed. Extermination and labour camps were therefore set up throughout Europe in order to exterminate the estimated eleven million European Jews.

To begin with, the Nazis rounded-up all the Jews living across Europe. They were able to do this quite easily because many Jews were already living in ghettos (such as the one in Warsaw). The Nazis told the Jews that they were going to be re-settled to a more pleasant location. Jews were told to pack some of their belongings and leave their ghettos. Many did not question the Nazis because they had received postcards from members of their families who were already in these 'new locations'.

Jews were herded onto trains which ran along specially constructed railway lines. The trains took them to extermination and labour camps across Europe – such as Belzec, Buchenwald, Sobibor and Treblinka. The train journeys, which sometimes took several days, were very uncomfortable. Many people were crammed into a very small space and had to go without food and water.

SOURCE B

Many Jews being taken to concentration camp had to travel in extreme discomfort. This photograph shows several people crowded into a freight truck, 1942.

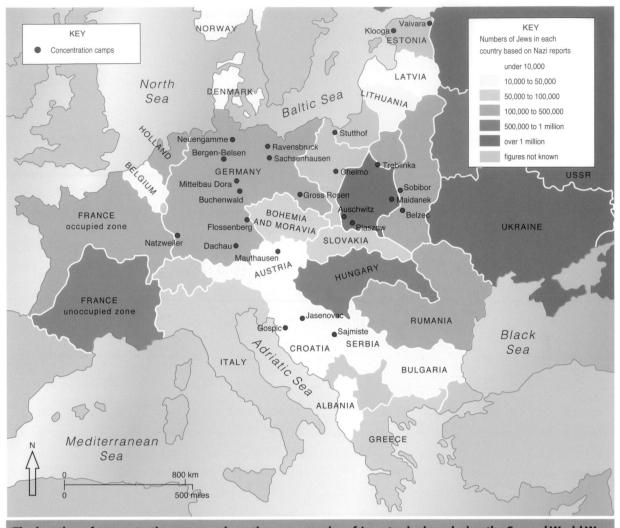

KEY

● Concentration camps

KEY
Numbers of Jews in each country based on Nazi reports

under 10,000
10,000 to 50,000
50,000 to 100,000
100,000 to 500,000
500,000 to 1 million
over 1 million
figures not known

NORWAY

North Sea

DENMARK

Baltic Sea

ESTONIA
Vaivara ●
Klooga ●

LATVIA

LITHUANIA

USSR

Neuengamme ●
Bergen-Belsen ●
● Ravensbruck
● Sachsenhausen
GERMANY
Mittelbau Dora ●
Buchenwald ●
● Gross Rosen
Flossenberg ●
Natzweiler ●
Dachau ●

HOLLAND

BELGIUM

Stutthof ●

● Chelmo
● Treblinka
● Sobibor
Auschwitz ● ● Maidanek
● Belzec
● Piaszow

BOHEMIA AND MORAVIA

SLOVAKIA

UKRAINE

FRANCE occupied zone

FRANCE unoccupied zone

Mauthausen ●

AUSTRIA

HUNGARY

RUMANIA

Black Sea

● Jasenovac
Gospic ●
● Sajmiste
CROATIA   SERBIA

Adriatic Sea

ITALY

BULGARIA

ALBANIA

GREECE

Mediterranean Sea

N

0   800 km
0   500 miles

The location of concentration camps where the mass murder of Jews took place during the Second World War.

Key words

Slav A person who speaks the Slavonic language.

SOURCE C

We were taken to a train station, put into groups of 60 and crowded into freight cars. Each of us was given a bucket to use as a toilet. We wondered where we were going and how long the journey would last. It was difficult to see outside because there was only a small window.

An account given by Errikos Sevillias, who was rounded-up by the Nazis and sent to Auschwitz-Birkenau.

Auschwitz-Birkenau concentration camp

The largest and most notorious Nazi concentration camp was Auschwitz-Birkenau in Poland. Around 1.5 million people died here. Jews, gypsies, **Slavs** and homosexuals from all across Europe were sent there.

Arriving at Auschwitz-Birkenau

Many people being sent to Auschwitz-Birkenau were unaware of what was waiting for them there. The Nazis had told them that they were being re-housed and would be given land and jobs.

When they arrived at Auschwitz-Birkenau, the men, women and children were separated. They were told to form two queues. People who appeared healthy and strong were put into one queue – these people would work. The remainder – those who were too young, too old, or too weak to work – were sent to die.

💡 *Why did there appear to be so little panic amongst those arriving at Auschwitz-Birkenau?*

💡 *Look at the map on page 139. Auschwitz-Birkenau was the largest and most frequently used concentration camp. Why do you think this was?*

What was life really like in Auschwitz-Birkenau?

Look at Sources D to M about life in the Auschwitz-Birkenau concentration camp.

Look at the map on page 139.

SOURCE D

In most cases the new arrivals did not know what awaited them. They were invited to undress for showers. The shower rooms had clothes hooks, benches and so on. But they were really gas chambers in disguise.

From a modern textbook.

SOURCE E

One evening as I was on my way to visit friends, I noticed a group of women standing round a huge wooden tub. They pushed me away. But I had time to see what they were doing. Tiny fingers were grasping the edge of the tub. In order to save mothers who had secretly given birth, these women were drowning the infants. They told each mother that they knew a place where her child could be put away that was safe. Only in this way could the mothers carry on working, which was essential if they were not to be sent straight to the gas chamber.

Claudette Kennedy.

SOURCE F

A drawing of the Auschwitz-Birkenau concentration camp by a Holocaust survivor.

SOURCE G

They punched me until I was in a state of collapse. I was eventually locked into a barrack full of people who had been selected to be taken to the gas chambers. Realising the consequences, I was determined to escape and managed to climb out at night through a narrow window with a colleague.

An account by a Holocaust survivor, Victor Greenberg.

SOURCE H

We had to wait in queue for our turn, all of us nervous and terrified and trying to keep out of the way of the German soldiers. I realised that the Germans were separating people into rows – one row to the left and the other to the right. I saw the left-hand row was full of children and old people, and I knew that I must avoid it at all costs.

Arek Hersh describes his experience of arriving at Auschwitz-Birkenau.

SOURCE I

A photograph showing daily life in the concentration camp.

SOURCE J

The selection process on the railway platform at Auschwitz-Birkenau, showing two different queues, summer 1944.

SOURCE K

My twin sister Rachel and I were eleven years old. Both of us cried when we were separated from our mother and brother. Then a woman who had been in Auschwitz for a long time came over to us and said: 'Do not cry children. You see, they are burning your parents'.

Vera Blau, a Holocaust survivor, describes her experiences at Auschwitz-Birkenau.

SOURCE L

When one woman was ordered to undress completely she threw her shoe in the SS guard's face, grabbed his revolver and shot him in the stomach. After her act of defiance, other women began to strike the SS men at the very entrance of the gas chamber, severely injuring two of them.

Jerzy Tabau, a non-Jewish Polish prisoner at Auschwitz, speaking in a report in October 1943.

A photograph showing prisoners putting a dead body into a cremation oven at a concentration camp.

SOURCE N

There were many Jewish doctors living in our section of the camp – women doctors, men doctors, eye doctors, ear doctors. Mengele came to speak to them every day and gave them orders to what to do with each twin.

Magda Speigel, survivor of Auschwitz. Josef Mengele was a Nazi scientist who carried out horrific experiments on inmates in the name of 'science'. Many of his experiments involved twins.

TASKS...

1 a) Copy the chart below.

Statement	Evidence for	Evidence against	Should the statement be changed? If yes, how?
No children survived the selection process.			
No one ever tried to escape from Auschwitz-Birkenau.			
No one knew what was happening at Auschwitz-Birkenau.			
People only died in the gas chambers at Auschwitz-Birkenau.			
Hard manual work was the only type of job that the prisoners at Auschwitz-Birkenau were allowed to do.			

b) Now read the different survivor accounts and evaluate the images on pages 140–2 to complete your chart. **WS**

2 Why do you think so few men, women and children survived the Auschwitz-Birkenau concentration camp?

Plenary

If you had to choose one source to help other people understand what happened at Auschwitz-Birkenau, which one would you choose? Why? Share your opinion with the rest of the class.

HOW SHOULD WE REMEMBER THE HOLOCAUST TODAY?

Objectives

In this section you will find out:
- why it is important to learn about the Holocaust
- how we should remember the Holocaust.

To investigate these ideas you will:
- discuss how books, films and events help us to remember the Holocaust
- write an assembly to commemorate the Holocaust.

Starter

SOURCE A

It is not what has happened, but what has been prevented from ever taking place, the sum of all unwritten books, thoughts unthought, of unfelt feelings, of works never accomplished, of lives unlived to their natural end.

Paulina Preis writing in 1969.

💡 *Why do you think it is important to be taught about the Holocaust?*

💡 *In pairs, discuss the different ways in which you think the Holocaust could be remembered.*

Key words

Commemorate To preserve the memory of something, often by a public act.

What happened to European Jews after the Second World War?

The liberation of the camps

As the Second World War ended, the concentration and extermination camps were liberated by the Soviet, American or British armies. What they discovered in the camps was extremely disturbing. Thousands of corpses had been thrown into shallow graves and dead bodies were heaped together in piles. Those people who were still alive were so weak they could hardly speak or move.

Female prison guards at the Bergen-Belsen concentration camp in Germany are made to bury the bodies of those people they helped to kill.

Liberation of the camps did not end the suffering of Jewish people. Most survivors had seen family and friends die in awful circumstances. They did not know who they could trust anymore. Nor did they have any links with their old lives, after years of segregation and the changes that occurred as a result of the anti-Semitic laws in Germany.

The problems Jews faced

The survivors of the Holocaust faced many problems. Where could they go? What could they do? Were any of their family or friends still alive? Who would be punished for the Holocaust?

Many of the survivors felt guilty that they had survived whereas others had died. Their will to live deteriorated and many ex-prisoners could not cope. They were unable to eat properly, because for years they hadn't been given enough food. Their bodies were so badly damaged that they found it hard to fight off disease.

Organisations were set up to help Jewish survivors of the Holocaust find lost relatives and re-build their lives. Many Jews left Europe to start new lives in other countries, for example the USA or Australia. Others went to the newly established Jewish homeland in Israel in 1948. Some Jews even returned to their old towns and villages in Europe, so that they could stay in touch with their own heritage and live in a familiar environment.

Remembering the Holocaust

It is more than 50 years since the atrocities of the Holocaust became known worldwide. Approximately six million Jews died during the Holocaust. There have been many discussions about whether we should remember the event, how we should commemorate it and how we can honour those who died.

Advertisement for The Pianist, a film about Holocaust made in 2002.

A Holocaust survivor talking to a group of people about his experiences.

Yad Vashem Holocaust memorial in Jerusalem, Israel.

TASKS...

1 Look at Sources C to E. How do you think these things help people today to learn about and remember the Holocaust? Discuss this question with a partner.

2 National Holocaust Day in the UK was introduced in 2001. Write a brief outline for a school assembly to take place on National Holocaust Day. You may include images and poems if you wish. You must be able to explain why you have included the information. Use the following table to help you plan what you will include.

Time	Resource included	Commentary about the resource	Reasons for inclusion

3 Share your assembly ideas with the rest of your class. What have you agreed on and what have you disagreed on? What do you think makes a good assembly?

Plenary

Look back to the facts about the Holocaust on page 125. What three extra statements would you now include? Give reasons for your choice.

RIGHTS AND FREEDOMS: CONCLUSION

In this section you have studied many examples of how rights and freedoms have been restricted and how people have resisted these restrictions. Copy out and complete the following mind map to show how much you have learned.

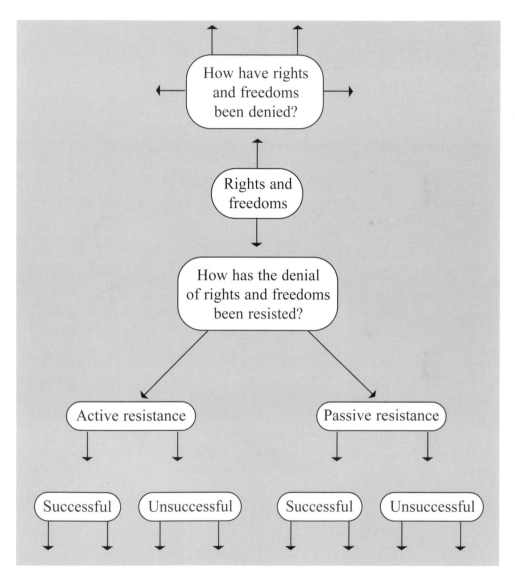

Why type of resistance has acheived the greatest success – active or passive resistance? Hold a class debate and vote on this question.

THEME: THE CHANGING NATURE OF WARFARE IN THE TWENTIETH CENTURY

INTRODUCTION

In this section you will study events from the three major conflicts of the twentieth century – the First World War, the Second World War and the Cold War. These conflicts changed the world and affected millions of lives in many different ways.

SOURCE A

British troops at the Somme, a scene from a British government film, The Battle of the Somme, released in August 1916.

SOURCE B

The bombing of London during the Second World War, December 1940.

SOURCE C

The Berlin Wall, 1962.

WHY DO WARS HAPPEN?

DO ALL WARS HAVE THE SAME CAUSES?

8

Objectives

In this section you will find out:
- what can cause wars to happen
- why the First World War started
- why tension in Europe was increasing before 1914.

To investigate these ideas you will:
- create a mind map linking the causes of the First World War to the five themes you have studied
- use information to predict outcomes
- consider the strengths and weaknesses of contemporary accounts.

Starter

Wars happen for many different reasons. In pairs, try to think of at least three reasons why one country might go to war with another. Share your reasons with others in your class. Create a class mind map showing all the reasons you have thought of. Do any of your reasons link to the common causes of war explained below?

Common causes of war

In the following sections, you will study the causes of the three major wars of the twentieth century:

- the First World War (1914–18)
- the Second World War (1939–45)
- the Cold War (1945–90).

As you study each conflict, you may identify some common themes that played a part in causing each war. These themes are explained below.

Militarism – when countries race to build up their armies, navies, weapons and strategies to defend against attack or to attack others.

Imperialism – when countries try to build large empires by conquering other countries.

Ideology – a set of beliefs that may determine the way a country is run and the way the people are allowed to live.

Alliances – the agreements countries make to be friends and to support each other.

Nationalism – when one country thinks it is better than others and feels very patriotic (proud and loyal) to the country.

WHAT WERE THE CAUSES OF THE FIRST WORLD WAR?

'I heard that the First World War started when a bloke called Archie Duke shot an ostrich because he was hungry.'

'I think you mean it started when the Archduke of Austria-Hungary got shot.'

'No, there was definitely an ostrich involved.'

'The real reason for the whole thing was that it was too much effort not to have a war.'

A conversation from the BBC comedy series, Blackadder Goes Forth, 1989.

💡 What questions would you ask about this conversation?

💡 Can you think of any problems in using comedy programmes as historical evidence? Give reasons for your answer.

The first major conflict of the twentieth century was the First World War, which began in 1914 and lasted for four years. By the end of this section you will be able to work out how accurate Source A is as an explanation of the causes of the First World War.

Tension in Europe was increasing in the years before 1914 for many different reasons. There was a great deal of hatred and rivalry between nations, and these problems were the long-term causes of the First World War. The main problems are shown on page 151–2.

A map showing Europe in 1900.

- Germany was trying to increase the size of its empire to provide raw materials for industry and to show it was as powerful as Britain.
- In 1839 Britain signed an agreement with Belgium promising to help if Belgium was attacked by Germany.
- In 1871 Germany took the border region of Alsace-Lorraine from French control during the Franco–Prussian War. France wanted revenge for this.
- In 1882 Germany, Italy and Austria-Hungary formed a military alliance called the Triple Alliance. They promised to help each other if attacked.
- In 1905 the Germans formed the Schlieffen Plan, which contained their strategy for fighting Russia and France. (In the event of a war, Germany would be surrounded by these enemy countries.)

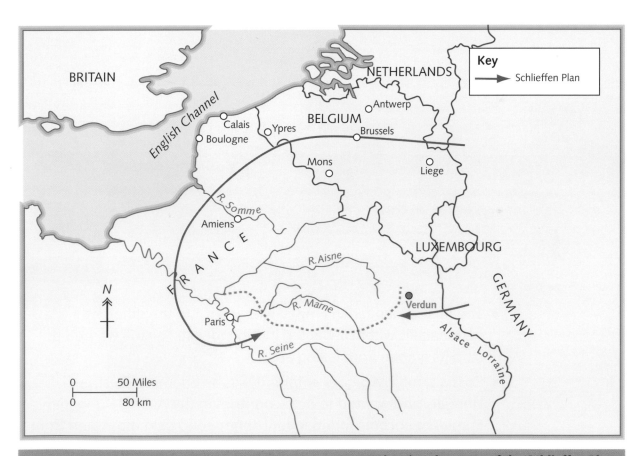

A map showing the route of the Schlieffen Plan.

The German plan was to advance through Belgium (a **neutral** country) and invade France quickly before fighting Russia, which would take longer. This meant that if Germany went to war against Russia, it would have to declare war on France or the Schlieffen Plan would not work.

Key words

Neutral Not taking sides.

- In 1906 Britain launched the first *Dreadnought*, the most modern and effective warship of its time. It was quicker and carried bigger guns than other ships.

- In 1907 Germany wanted to increase the strength of its navy, so it launched its own version of the *Dreadnought* (the *Nassau Class*) to compete with Britain. An arms race between Britain and Germany began.

A Dreadnought battleship.

- The Austro-Hungarian Empire was weak and the different nationalities within it wanted independence. Austria wanted to stop its empire from falling apart.

- Russia wanted a bigger empire. It was an enemy of Austria-Hungary and wanted to help countries in the Austro-Hungarian Empire to become independent. It hoped to gain more land from this.

- Serbia wanted to unite all the Slav people in the Austro-Hungarian Empire. There was a large Serb population in Russia, and Russia wanted to help Serbia achieve its aims at Austria's expense.

- In 1907 France, Russia and Britain signed the Triple Entente, which stated they would help each other if attacked.

TASKS...

1 Work in pairs or small groups to create a large mind map showing the causes of the First World War.

   a) On a large piece of paper, plot the five main themes of war (the themes you looked at on page 149 as shown below.

   b) Now study the information on pages 151–2 which shows the tensions in Europe leading up to the First World War. Think which tensions might have been a cause of war.

   c) Decide for each point which theme on your diagram it relates to. Write the point on to the mind map under the correct heading, stating clearly why it could cause war.

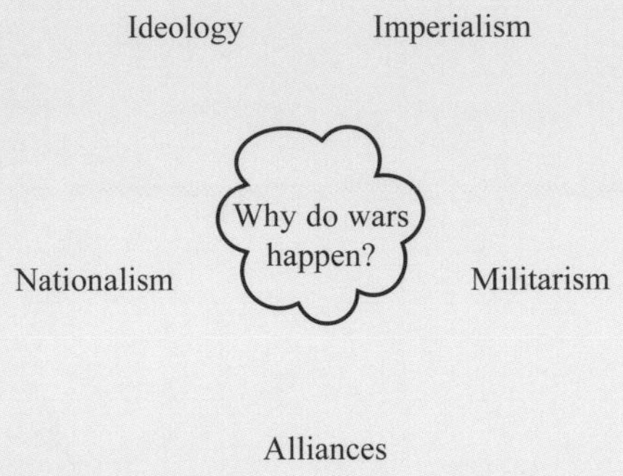

Ideology   Imperialism

Why do wars happen?

Nationalism   Militarism

Alliances

   d) You might think that some of the causes on your diagram link to more than one theme. If so, draw an arrow to link the cause to the second theme. Over the top of the arrow explain why it links to this theme as well.

2 When you have finished, compare your diagram with that of another group to see if your diagrams are similar. Explain the decisions you made to the other group.

Short-term causes of the First World War

In 1914 tension in Europe reached its peak and the spark for war came in the form of a murder.

NEWSFLASH!   28 June 1914

The Austrian Prince, Archduke Franz Ferdinand, has been murdered in Sarajevo, the capital of Bosnia.

Archduke Ferdinand was today visiting Sarajevo with his wife, Countess Sophie, to celebrate their wedding anniversary. They were also there to inspect the Bosnian army, which is part of the Austro-Hungarian Empire.

The murder was carried out by a young Serbian terrorist called Gavrilo Princip. He fired two shots into the car in which the Archduke and his wife were travelling. Princip was arrested shortly afterwards. He belongs to a Serbian terrorist group known as the Black Hand, which wants Bosnia to be free from Austrian control.

Austria have blamed the Serbian government for the assassination.

Use your knowledge of Europe in 1914 to work out how this murder in Sarajevo caused the First World War.

The outbreak of war in Europe

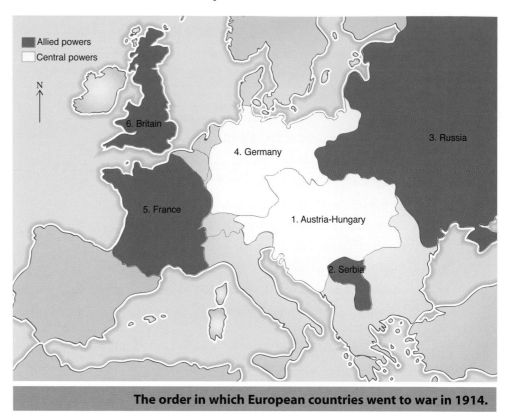

The order in which European countries went to war in 1914.

TASKS...

1   Look at the map which shows the order in which the countries of Europe went to war in 1914. The colours show who was fighting whom (the Allies versus the Central Powers).

   a) Use the details from the mind map which you started on page 153 to try to work out why each country joined the war in the order it did.

   💡 **Clue:** the information about the Alliances and the Schlieffen Plan will help you, though you will need to consider a few other points too.

   Add details about the murder of the Archduke to the appropriate place on your mind map.

   b) Now try to work out why the murder of the Archduke Franz Ferdinand sparked the First World War. Write a paragraph or draw a flowchart to show this, explaining why you think each country got involved.

2   What do you think was the most important cause of the First World War? Do you think the long-term causes or the short-term triggers played the biggest part in making war happen in 1914.

Plenary

Do you agree with the quote from *Blackadder* on page 150? Explain why.

WHAT WERE THE CAUSES OF THE SECOND WORLD WAR?

In this section you will find out:
- how the results of the First World War helped to cause the Second World War
- whether the Second World War could have been avoided
- why the Second World War broke out.

To investigate these ideas you will:
- organise evidence on a mind map linking to the themes you have studied
- take part in a decision-making activity
- design a flow chart.

Starter

Some historians have argued that the results of the First World War helped to cause the Second World War. Look back at the map of Europe in 1914 on page 154. Then look at the map below.

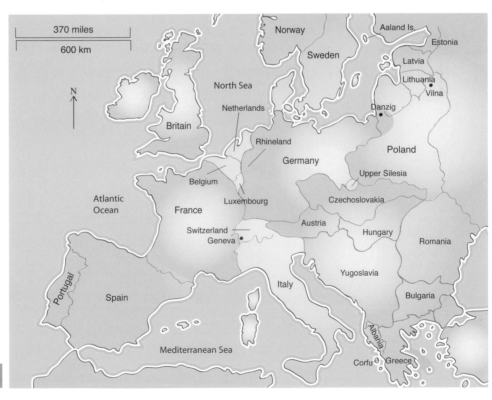

Europe in 1919.

List the differences you notice between Europe in 1914 and Europe in 1919.

💡 *Which country do you think would be most upset by the changes that had taken place? Explain why.*

💡 *Can you think why these changes might have taken place? Discuss your thoughts with a partner.*

💡 *Can you think of any reasons why the First World War helped to cause the Second World War?*

The effects of the First World War

In 1918, after four years of fighting, the German army surrendered at 11 am on 11 November. The First World War was over.

In 1919 the victorious leaders of the Allied countries (Britain, France and the USA) met to discuss the future of Europe. They met at the Palace of Versailles in France. Their main concern was how best to deal with the defeated enemy, Germany.

The results of this meeting were written down in the Treaty of Versailles, which was signed by the leaders on 28 June 1919. Germany had no say in the treaty, and was forced to accept its harsh and humiliating terms. According to the treaty, Germany had to:

- accept full blame for starting the First World War
- pay reparations (compensation) of £6600 million for the destruction and damage caused by the war
- give up possession of its overseas colonies
- give up territory in Europe
- reduce its military power:
  - reduce the German army to just 100,000 men
  - give up its airforce and submarines
  - reduce the size of its navy to just six battleships.

SOURCE Ⓐ

As a soldier, I cannot help feeling that it were better to perish honourably than accept a disgraceful peace.

Field-Marshal Von Hindenburg, Germany's supreme commander in the First World War, speaking in June 1919.

TASKS...

1   Make a list of adjectives that a German person might use to describe the Treaty of Versailles.

2   Using all the information in this section, explain why many historians believe that the Treaty of Versailles was an important cause of the Second World War.

Could the Second World War have been avoided?

The Treaty of Versailles was very unpopular with the German people. Germans felt betrayed by the government that had signed the treaty and thereby accepted its harsh terms.

A photograph showing Germans queuing in Hanover to register for unemployment benefit in 1930.

There were economic problems in Germany in the early 1920s as the government struggled to pay the reparations set at Versailles. As a result many extreme political groups sprang up. One of these was the Nazi Party, which was led by Adolf Hitler.

In 1929 there was a severe worldwide economic depression. The economic crisis hit Germany very hard. By 1932 six million German people were out of work; many people were hungry and homeless.

During these difficult times people lost even more faith in the German government and began to look for an alternative. In 1933 Hitler was voted leader of Germany. He promised to make Germany wealthy, powerful and proud again, as Sources C to G show.

Unsere letzte Hoffnung: HITLER

'Our last hope: Hitler' – a Nazi poster used in the 1932 election campaign, which targets the unemployed.

WHY DO WARS HAPPEN?

157

A Nazi election poster of 1928. It says the sacrifices made by Germany in the First World War were in vain.

The Nazis promised to restore Germany's status and secure strong government and national unity. These were powerful messages to people who were desperate for answers.

Hitler established a reputation as a rousing public speaker who captivated his audiences. He toured the country delivering speeches to ever larger audiences. He kept his message simple and found something to offer all sections of German society.

A modern historian writing in 2003.

A Nazi election poster of 1932. It says 'Women! Millions of men out of work! Millions of children without a future! Save our German families. Vote for Adolf Hitler!'

Hitler appealed to the nation as a whole. He declared that Germans deserved to live with pride in a new nation free from the burdens imposed by the Treaty of Versailles and safe from people he believed to be inferior such as the Jews.

He also appealed to different sections of society. The working classes were promised jobs and farmers would receive state aid. German businesses would be protected. Since over half of the population were women, Hitler was keen to stress the role women would play in Nazi Germany. The Nazis portrayed themselves as the party of family values.

An extract from a modern history textbook.

TASKS...

1 Look at Sources C to G, which illustrate Hitler's promises to the German people. **WS**

   a) For each source, write down why you think the promise might appeal to people in Germany in 1933.

   b) Share your ideas with a partner.

2 Now look at the promises again and split them into three groups:
   - those that would *not* cause war
   - those that *might* cause war
   - those that would *definitely* cause war.

3 Which promise do you think would have won Hitler the most votes? Explain your answer.

4 Look again at the five themes of war on page 149 and create a mind map, like the one you filled in for the First World War (see page 153), to show the causes of the Second World War. Decide under which theme each of Hitler's promises should go and write them on your mind map. You only need to do this for the promises that you have decided might or would definitely cause war.

5 Do you think there are any links or similarities between Hitler's promises and the causes of the First World War? Discuss this in small groups and then as a class.

Why did the Second World War break out?

Once Hitler became leader of Germany, he began to act on his promises. This started a sequence of events that led to war in 1939. Some people have said that Britain and France should have acted sooner against Hitler to stop him. When you have read the information on the following pages, you'll be asked whether you agree or not.

TASKS...

1 In pairs, imagine you are advisers to the British government between 1933 and 1939. For each of Hitler's actions described on pages 160–1, decide what advice you would give to your government on how to respond. You may choose from the options given for each situation or make up your own advice. Remember to take into account the information in the thought bubbles for each situation.

SITUATION ONE

After becoming leader of Germany in 1933, Hitler begins to re-arm and to build up the German army and air force. At first, he does this in secret. However, it soon becomes clear to the British government that Germany is rearming. What action should Britain take?

Three options:

a) Attack Germany and destroy the weapons that have been built.

b) Do nothing.

c) Compromise with Hitler on an agreed limit on what he can do.

What might the British government think?

Hitler is breaking the terms of the Treaty of Versailles.

Hitler should be stopped before he gets too strong.

Maybe we should allow this. The Soviet Union is a greater threat than Nazi Germany. Hitler could help us to fight them, if necessary.

SITUATION TWO

It is 1936. Hitler sends his troops into the Rhineland, which had been demilitarised by the Treaty of Versailles. What action should the British government take?

Three options:

a) Send an army to the Rhineland to stop Hitler.

b) Allow Hitler to keep troops there.

c) Send a message to Hitler that you disapprove of what he is doing.

What might the British government think?

The Rhineland is a demilitarised zone. Hitler is breaking the Treaty of Versailles by having troops there.

The Rhineland is German territory. Maybe it's only fair for the Germans to have troops there.

The German army is not very big. Maybe Hitler should be stopped now, before the army gets any bigger.

SITUATION THREE

It is 1938. Hitler has just announced that Germany is to unite with Austria (the *Anschluss*) after sending his troops into Austria. The *Anschluss* is forbidden by the Treaty of Versailles. What action should the British government take?

Three options:

a) Do nothing and allow the *Anschluss* to continue.

b) Tell Hitler to cancel the *Anschluss* or risk war.

c) Ask the Austrian government if it wants the *Anschluss* or not, then make a decision.

What might the British government think?

People in Britain do not want another war after the horrors of the First World War.

Hitler is continuing to break the terms of the Treaty of Versailles .

Hitler says that he wants peace. Maybe he will stop if he is allowed to unite with Austria.

There are lots of German-speaking people in Austria. Why stop the Anschluss if people in Austria want it? There may be no harm in Germany and Austria uniting.

SITUATION FOUR

It is September 1938. Hitler has demanded that the Sudetenland, which became part of Czechoslovakia after the First World War, should be returned to Germany. What should the British government do?

Three options:

a) Ask the Czech government what they want and then decide what to do.

b) Allow Hitler to have the Sudetenland, although he must agree to leave the rest of Czechoslovakia alone.

c) Declare war on Germany.

What might the British government think?

Most of the people in the Sudetenland are German speaking and want to reunite with Germany.

The Czech government is worried that Hitler will not stop at the Sudetenland and will take the rest of Czechoslovakia.

The British people do not want to go to war with Germany.

Hitler is continuing to break the Treaty of Versailles.

SITUATION FIVE

It is March 1939. Hitler's troops have invaded the rest of Czechoslovakia. What action should the British government take?

Three options:

a) Do nothing to help Czechoslovakia.

b) Declare war on Germany to help the Czechs.

c) Threaten Hitler with war if he invades another country (you think he might invade Poland next).

What might the British government think?

Britain and France need more time to prepare for war against Hitler.

Hitler has broken all his promises and must be stopped!

Czechoslovakia needs help. It cannot fight Hitler alone.

SITUATION SIX

It is the 1 September 1939. Hitler has invaded Poland, demanding the return of land (the Polish corridor) that had been taken from Germany by the Treaty of Versailles. What should the British government do?

Two options:

a) Do nothing, and hope that Hitler will stop invading other countries now that he has the Polish corridor.

b) Declare war on Germany.

What might the British government think?

Hitler seems to be trying to take over Europe. He must be stopped.

Hitler's promises mean nothing. He clearly does not want peace and force is the only way to stop him.

Hitler is just trying to take back what he feels belongs to Germany. Maybe we should just cancel the Treaty of Versailles.

What did Britain do?

What the British and French governments actually did in each situation was to follow a policy called appeasement. The aim was to avoid war if at all possible by giving in to Hitler's demands on the condition that Hitler made certain guarantees towards peace. It was hoped that by giving Hitler what he wanted, war would be avoided. However, the policy of appeasement is generally seen to have failed because each time Hitler made a promise he later broke it.

There was a lot of support for the policy of appeasement in Britain because people wanted to avoid another war like the First World War with its massive losses of life and damage.

TASKS...

1 a) Draw a flow chart to summarise the road to war between 1933 and 1939. On it you should show the actions Hitler took and the reactions of the allies. **WS**

   b) Look at your flow chart. Can you see how one thing led to another? Do you think that the Second World War could have been avoided? Write several paragraphs to answer this question using the information in this section. Use the following guidelines to help you.

   • Write one paragraph to explain how the Second World War might have been avoided if the allies have acted sooner against Hitler.

   • Your next paragraph should explain why the Second World War might have been unavoidable because of Hitler's actions and beliefs.

   • Write a short conclusion that explains your overall opinion about whether the Second World War could have been avoided based on the evidence you have studied.

2 Look at the mind map you created for the Second World War (page 159). Add details about the causes of the Second World War near to the appropriate themes on the map.

Plenary

What do you think was the most important cause of the Second World War – the Treaty of Versailles, Adolf Hitler's actions, or the policy of appeasement? Explain your answer carefully.

Can you spot any links or similarities between the causes of the First and Second World Wars?

WHAT WERE THE CAUSES OF THE COLD WAR?

Objectives

In this section you will find out:

- why the USA and the Soviet Union became enemies after 1945
- how the results of the Second World War helped to cause the Cold War.

To investigate these ideas you will:

- classify information to show the differences between communism and capitalism
- prepare two radio reports and complete a mind map linking the causes of the Cold War to the five themes you have been studying.

Starter

Look at Source A.

Damage at Hiroshima after the explosion of an atomic bomb on 6 August 1945.

Source A shows the destruction of a Japanese city, Hiroshima, by a US nuclear bomb at the end of the Second World War.

💡 *Do you think the creation of nuclear weapons has made war more or less likely to break out in the future? Discuss this question with a partner and then with your class.*

The background to the Cold War

When Germany and Japan were defeated in 1945, the Second World War ended. The USA and the Soviet Union came out of the war as the strongest nations in the world – the wealthiest countries with the biggest armies. They were known as the superpowers.

The Cold War is the name given to the rivalry and tension between the two superpowers. There was never any direct fighting although there remained an atmosphere of distrust and hostility between the two countries. By 1950 both the USA and the Soviet Union had nuclear weapons. This meant a 'hot' war between them was less likely, as it would result in total destruction for both sides. Therefore a Cold War of words, **propaganda** and threats developed.

One of the main reasons why the USA and the Soviet Union were enemies was because they had different ideas about how a country should be run.

Key words

Propaganda Information used to persuade people to believe a particular point of view.

Capitalist A supporter of capitalism, an economic system based on private ownership of business, property and industry.

Communist A supporter of communism, a system based on all industry and property being owned by the state and shared for the good of everyone.

The United States of America

The USA was a **capitalist** country that believed in:

- a number of political parties
- the private ownership of businesses
- the private ownership of property
- individual people working hard to make their own wealth – the government should not have to provide for its people.

The Soviet Union

The Soviet Union was a **communist** country that believed in:

- one political party
- businesses owned and run by the government
- property owned by the government
- a classless society with no individual profit – profits are used for the good of all people.

TASKS...

1 John lives in capitalist USA and Alexander lives in the communist Soviet Union. Below are some statements made by either John or Alexander about their life. Decide who would have said which statement.

Capitalist John

a) People are free to vote for rulers of their choice. There are at least two political parties and elections are held every five years.

b) I work hard to make money for our country. People not truly be free until they are equal. Otherwise freedom is just for the rich.

c) I can travel outside of my own country with special permission. But the government should use its resources to provide for the people - thats more important than going on holiday.

d) I own my own shop and can decide what to stock and how much to charge for the things I sell. In this way, I am able to make a financial profit.

e) The newspapers tell me if the government has made a mistake or done something unpopular.

f) People can vote for the one political party that will truly take care of their interests.

g) Our system is based on equality. The state owns all business and its people work hard to make the country richer. Only the greedy want to keep the profits for themselves.

h) The government owns the newspapers, because everything belongs to the state. The newspapers tell me what the government is doing to look after the people.

i) I own a three-bedroomed house. I can sell my house whenever I want and move to a different part of the country.

j) I work hard to make money for myself. People should be free to earn as much money as they can make through their own efforts.

k) Under our system there is no private ownership of property. The government owns all property and uses its resources to provide for the people.

l) I can go on holiday whenever I like. The money I earn enables me to pay for the expensive holidays abroad.

Communist Alexander

2 What do you think John would have thought of Alexander's way of life? In pairs, jot down some ideas.

3 What do you think Alexander would have thought of John's way of life? In pairs, jot down some ideas.

4 How do you think the differences that you have identified between capitalism and communism contributed towards the Cold War? Discuss your ideas as a class.

How did the Cold War start?

Soviet expansion

During the Second World War the Soviet Union and the USA had been allies. However, there was a history of mistrust between the countries. The problem was that both countries thought that their political system was the best way to run a country. The USA bitterly opposed communism and feared that the Soviet Union was trying to spread its beliefs across the world. Most Soviet politicians, however, thought that they were under threat from the capitalist countries of western Europe, especially Britain and France.

Between 1945 and 1948 the Soviet Union made sure that every country in Eastern Europe had a government that was both communist and sympathetic to the Soviet Union. This was in part a defensive measure – it would make invasion of the Soviet Union from the west more difficult.

The spread of communism in Eastern Europe after the Second World War.

💡 Why do you think that the USA and its Western allies were so worried by the Soviet Union's actions shown on the map?

The fall of the 'iron curtain'

Capitalist countries in the West, and the USA in particular, saw the spread of communism in Eastern Europe as a move by the Soviet Union towards world domination. They thought that their capitalist way of life was under threat, and feared the spread of communism to other countries. They were determined to stop communism from spreading any further.

In March 1946 the British prime minister, Winston Churchill, made a speech in which he referred to an 'iron curtain' coming down across Europe. By this he meant that Europe had been divided in half – with capitalist countries to the west, and communist countries to the east. Churchill argued that only people in the capitalist countries were really free; behind the 'iron curtain' the people in the communist countries were not free and had to do what their government dictated.

SOURCE B

PEEP UNDER THE IRON CURTAIN

A cartoon published in the Daily Mail in March 1946, commenting on Churchill's 'iron curtain' speech.

💡 What do you think the Soviet Union would have thought of Winston Churchill's 'iron curtain' speech?

TASKS...

1 Look at Source B. What do you think the cartoonist is saying about Churchill's speech?

2 How useful is Source B as evidence about the Cold War? Give reasons for your answer.

3 Draw another mind map like the ones you did for the First and Second World Wars (see pages 153 and 159). Add the causes of the Cold War you have discovered so far under the appropriate themes on the diagram.

How real was the threat of nuclear war during the Cold War?

TIMELINE
The arms race, 1945–60

1945 6 August: the USA drops the first ever **atomic bomb** on Hiroshima in Japan, causing mass destruction. The USA refuses to share its nuclear technology with the Soviet Union.

9 August: USA drops atomic bomb on Nagasaki in Japan.

1949 The Soviet Union successfully tests its own atomic bomb.

1952 The USA develops the **hydrogen bomb** (H–bomb).

1953 The Soviet Union develops a hydrogen bomb.

1955 The Soviet Union develops its own submarine-launched **nuclear missiles**.

1957 The Soviet Union begins developing nuclear missiles that can hit targets thousands of miles away.

1958 The USA begins development of long-range missiles.

1960 A US submarine launches a long-range missile from underneath the sea.

1960 Both the USA and the Soviet Union have enough nuclear weapons to destroy the population of the earth. This situation is known as Mutually Assured Destruction (MAD) and makes a 'hot' war less likely.

Key words

Atomic bomb A bomb in which atoms are split releasing tremendous energy.

Hydrogen bomb A bomb, more powerful than the atom bomb, in which hydrogen atoms give off tremendous energy.

Nuclear missile Any weapon that works by releasing energy created by the transformation of atoms.

TASKS...

1 **a)** What does the timeline tell you about another cause of tension between the two superpowers?

   b) Add this cause to your Cold War mind map.

2 During the Cold War there were lots of protests and campaigns against the existence of nuclear weapons. Using the theory of Mutually Assured Destruction (MAD), write a letter defending the existence of nuclear weapons as a way of preventing war.

How did the results of one war help to cause another?

Before the end of the Second World War the victorious allies (Britain, France, the USA and the Soviet Union) had to decide what to do with Germany, just as they had to at the end of the First World War.

Before the war had ended, each of the Allied powers agreed at the Yalta Conference of February 1945 that Germany was a threat to world peace. They agreed that Germany should be kept weak. The Allies decided to split Germany into four zones, to be controlled by Britain, France, the USA and the Soviet Union. The capital city of Germany, Berlin, fell into the Soviet zone, so Berlin was also split into four zones.

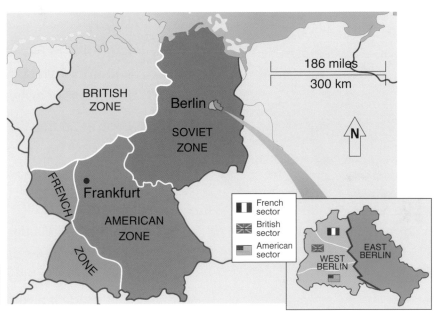

The division of Germany in 1945.

💡 Can you think of any possible problems with the division of Germany decided at the Yalta Conference in 1945?

💡 Can you think of a better solution for what to do with Germany? Explain your solution and why you think it is better.

By 1948 Britain, France and the USA had changed their minds about Germany. They decided that Germany should be strengthened to help protect against a bigger threat – the spread of communism from the Soviet Union. They put their three zones together and began to help the Germans strengthen their economy. Joseph Stalin, the leader of the Soviet Union, was furious about this and took action.

The Berlin Blockade

On 24 June 1948 Soviet troops cut off all road, rain and canal links between the West and Berlin. Stalin was trying to force the West out of Berlin. He planned to starve Berliners in the Western zone into submission. The USA considered using their army, but to have done so would have been seen as an act of war. The USA did not want to start a war with the Soviet Union.

💡 Imagine you are a Western adviser. How would you advise the West to deal with this problem? Remember, you do not want to give up Berlin and allow communism to spread, but you do not want to go to war with the Soviet Union.

Source C gives you a big clue as to how the West dealt with the Berlin blockade – the Allies decided to airlift food and supplies into Berlin.

💡 Why do you think that an airlift might allow the West to successfully keep control of Berlin and avoid a 'hot' war with the Soviet Union?
Discuss your answers as a class.

💡 Look at Source C. Do you think that Stalin will fire his gun? Why?

The Berlin airlift

During the Berlin airlift, 8000 tons of food, fuel and other items were flown from Western Germany into West Berlin every day. This made it a very expensive and difficult operation. Flying conditions were hazardous, causing accidents and the deaths of about 79 crew members. Soviet planes buzzed around the Western planes, but did not attack them.

On 12 May 1949 Stalin ended the blockade – it had lasted over 10 months. The Western Allies managed to save West Berlin, and so the capital of Germany remained divided between capitalism and communism. Following the blockade,

THE BIRD WATCHER

A Punch cartoon of July 1948 about the Berlin Blockade, titled 'The Bird Watcher'. The man holding the gun is Stalin.

Germany was split into two different countries – West Germany and East Germany. East Germany, which included East Berlin, was completely controlled by the communist Soviet Union. West Berlin remained a capitalist base in communist Eastern Europe.

TASKS...

1 It is 12 May 1949 and Stalin has ended the Berlin Blockade.

   a) In pairs, prepare two radio reports about the Berlin crisis. One of you will report for British radio; one of you will report for Soviet radio. Both of you have to claim that the Berlin Blockade was victory for your country, so your justification of victory will differ.
   Use the following guidelines to help you write your reports.

   - Briefly introduce your report by saying who you are (make up a name), who you are reporting for and what you are reporting about.
   - Next you need to outline what has been happening in Berlin. Try to describe the events and countries involved in such a way as to make it clear whose side you are on. For example, a British reporter might describe Stalin's blockade as *illegal/unjust/desperate/underhand*, whereas the airlift might be described as *heroic/glorious/brave/honourable*.
   - However, a Soviet reporter might describe Stalin's blockade as *justified/clever/courageous/legitimate*, whereas the airlift might be described as *cowardly/hopeless/foolhardy/expensive*.
   - Use relevant connectives to sequence your description of events: *later, meanwhile, because, however, nevertheless*.
   - Finally, you need to show your country's judgement about who 'won' with some (biased) evidence that 'proves' why your country won. You will need to use persuasive connectives: *in fact, therefore, this shows, undoubtedly*.

   b) When you have finished your broadcasts, present them to others in the class. As a pair, you should make sure that you have clearly shown how the British and the Soviets would interpret events differently.

2 Write a short paragraph to explain how the results of the Second World War contributed towards the Cold War.

NATO and the Warsaw Pact

As a result of the Berlin Blockade, the North Atlantic Treaty Organisation (NATO) was formed in 1949. This was a military alliance of European capitalist countries plus Canada and the USA. When NATO was expanded in 1955 to include West Germany, the Soviet Union responded by setting up its own military alliance, the Warsaw Pact.

Key
Members of
Warsaw Pact
Members of NATO

Members of NATO
The USA, Britain, Belgium, Canada, Denmark, France, Greece, Iceland, Italy, Luxembourg, the Netherlands, Norway, Portugal, Turkey, West Germany.

Members of The Warsaw Pact
The Soviet Union, Albania, Bulgaria, Czechoslovakia, East Germany, Hungary, Poland, Romania.

A map showing NATO and the Warsaw Pact.

TASKS...

1 Why do you think the existence of NATO and the Warsaw Pact was so dangerous? Think back to what happened in 1914.

2 Go back to the mind map you started on page 167. Add any further details you have discovered about the causes of Cold War.

3 Your mind maps should now be complete for the each of the three wars covered in this chapter. Look at them carefully. Then as a class discuss the similarities and differences you have discovered about the causes of these wars.

4 What are the most important points you have learned from the sections in this chapter about why wars happen? Explain your answer.

Plenary

WS Work in groups of three or four. Imagine you are producers for the BBC and have been given the following brief.

- You must produce a fifteen-minute historical documentary with the title, 'Why do wars happen?'
- You must focus on twentieth-century conflicts.
- You must make your audience aware of links between different conflicts and their causes.
- Your programme should be interesting, informative and imaginative.

Now create your documentary.

9

HOW AND WHY DID TWENTIETH CENTURY WARFARE CHANGE?

The twentieth century was a period when the way in which wars were fought changed dramatically. This was due to developments in technology that allowed new weapons and tactics to be introduced. These developments made killing the enemy easier and so wars became more destructive and deadly than ever before, affecting millions of people worldwide.

In this chapter you will compare warfare in three key conflicts of the twentieth century:

- the First World War
- the Second World War
- the Cold War.

You will look at some of the major battles and events that took place during the conflicts in order to answer the question 'How and why did twentieth century warfare change?'

WHAT HAPPENED DURING THE BATTLE OF THE SOMME?

Objectives

In this section you will find out:
- why the first day of the Battle of the Somme was such a disaster
- whether the Battle of the Somme was a complete failure for the British army.

To investigate these ideas you will:
- listen to and select details from a story
- show how some effects were more successful than others
- begin a comparison chart.

Starter

Read Sources A, B and C, which give different people's opinions about the preparations for the Battle of the Somme and the first day of battle (1 July 1916). Then answer the questions that follow.

SOURCE A

Key words

Artillery Weapons.

How did the planners imagine that British soldiers would get through the barbed wire? Who told them that **artillery** fire would pound such wire to pieces? Any soldier could have told them that shell fire lifts wire up and drops it down, often in a worse tangle than before.

Private George Coppard, a survivor of the Battle of the Somme.

The men are in splendid spirits. Several have said that they have never before been so well instructed and informed of the nature of the operation before them. The barbed wire has never been so well cut, nor the artillery preparation so thorough. All the commanders are full of confidence.

An extract from the British Commander-in-Chief's diary, dated 30 June 1916.

'Come on, we are ready for you.' These words appeared on several German placards above their **trenches** before the battle.

Reported in *The British Campaign in France and Flanders 1916*, by Sir Arthur Conan Doyle.

Key words

Trenches The protective ditches dug for soldiers fighting in battle.

 Which quote do you think is the odd one out? Why?

What was the Battle of the Somme about?

By 1916 the First World War had become a stalemate. Neither the Germans nor the British were making any real progress and conditions were getting even worse for the soldiers fighting in the trenches. It was in this situation that the Battle of the Somme was planned to try to break the deadlock and bring victory to Britain and its allies.

TASKS...

1 Read the story on pages 174–6 of what happened on 1 July 1916 – the first day of the Battle of the Somme. Get into groups of three. As you read the story:
- one of you should look out for any reasons for disaster linked to poor leadership and planning
- one of you should look out for any reasons for disaster linked to failing technology
- one of you should look out for any reasons for disaster linked to things beyond British control.

What happened on the first day of the Battle of the Somme?

The British launched an attack which they thought would defeat the Germans and bring about the end of the First World War. The attack had originally been planned as a joint British–French offensive. However, by 1916 the French were defending their fortress at Verdun in a very bloody battle, so the Battle of the Somme was left mainly to the British and their Commander-in-Chief, Field Marshall Douglas Haig. It was hoped that a successful attack would divert the Germans and relieve the pressure on the French at Verdun.

Haig was an experienced cavalry officer, but he sometimes underestimated the power of modern weapons. Haig's plan was to heavily bombard the German trenches for a week before the battle. This would destroy trenches, machine guns and artillery and kill the soldiers. The British troops would then simply walk in straight lines across **No Man's Land** and take over the German positions.

Unfortunately, this did not go to plan. To begin with, the Germans held the high ground around the Somme area. This meant they were able to see the British preparations for the bombardment. As a result they built a third line of trenches to strengthen their defences. British **reconnaissance** aircraft observed this, but Haig ignored their reports and warnings. He was determined to stick to his timetable for the attack and would not be delayed.

The Germans had also built deep **bunkers** about ten metres underground. During the bombardment they planned to move their weapons and soldiers into these bunkers to keep them safe.

The bombardment itself was intense. About 1.75 million shells were fired at the German positions and the front line trenches were almost totally destroyed. However, one-third of the **shells** were duds and did not explode. The second and third German defence lines remained intact and their troops were safe underground. The shells also failed to cut the huge belts of barbed wire that the British soldiers would need to get through as they advanced across No Man's Land.

At 7.25 am on 1 July 1916, the British guns stopped firing and 100,000 young volunteer soldiers, many of whom had never been in battle before, waited in their front line trenches for the order to advance. They were excited. They thought their task would be easy. Their commanders told them there couldn't possibly be any Germans left alive, and that they were about to become heroes.

In the German bunkers, the soldiers heard the British guns become quiet. Quickly they began to work, moving their machine-guns out of the bunkers to get them into position to face the advance of the British troops. They

Key words

Battalion A group of soldiers.

No Man's Land The land in between fighting armies.

Reconnaissance A survey of an area, often before battle.

Bunker An underground bomb-proof shelter.

Shells Explosives fired from large guns.

had practised this many times and could do it in less than five minutes.

At 7.30 am, the whistle blew and the first line of men went 'over the top', clambering through the gaps in the barbed wire into No Man's Land. A torrent of machine-gun fire swept along the lines as they advanced. The German machine-gunners concentrated their fire on the gaps in the barbed wire. This meant that many British soldiers were killed before they even got out of their trenches.

Despite this, the British continued to advance because no order was given to call off the attack until the end of the day. Wave after wave of British soldiers went 'over the top' – resulting in 35,000 being injured and 20,000 killed. Most of these deaths occurred in the first twenty minutes of the battle. None of the day's objectives were achieved.

British troops going 'over the top' on the first day of the Battle of the Somme, 1 July 1916.

The machine gun is a much over-rated weapon. Two per **battalion** is enough.

Field Marshall Douglas Haig speaking in 1915.

	Officers	Soldiers
Killed / died of wounds	993	18247
Wounded	1337	34156
Missing	96	2056
Taken prisoner	12	573
Total	**2438**	**55032**

British losses on the first day of the Battle of the Somme.

TASKS...

1 Before you read the story, you were asked to look for reasons for disaster in one particular area. Note down in your book all the reasons you can remember.

2 Get back into your group. Between you, copy and complete the chart below to show why the Battle of the Somme was such a disaster. Check your notes to make sure you have included all the reasons you were looking for.

Examples of poor leadership and planning	Examples of failing technology	Examples of things beyond British control

3 Look carefully at your completed chart. Are there any reasons that could be put under more than one heading? In your book, write a few sentences to say which reasons link to more than one category, and why.

Was the Battle of the Somme a complete failure?

After a disastrous start for British forces, the Battle of the Somme continued until it reached a deadlock on 30 November 1916. By that time, more than one million men had been killed during the battle. The map and Sources G to L will help you to assess whether the results of the battle were worth all the injuries and deaths.

SOURCE G

Ten of the tanks were hit by German artillery fire, nine broke down with mechanical difficulties and five failed to advance. But recognising the potential of the new weapon, Haig asked the War Office for 1000 more tanks. The Germans were far behind in their tank experiments.

A modern historian writes about what happened at the Somme in September 1916, when 45 British tanks went into battle for the first time.

SOURCE H

British	420,000
French	200,000
German	650,000

The casualty figures for the Battle of the Somme, 1916.

SOURCE J

SOURCE I

The Somme is the muddy grave of the German army.

Spoken by German General Paul von Hindenburg.

British troops at the Battle of the Somme in October 1916.

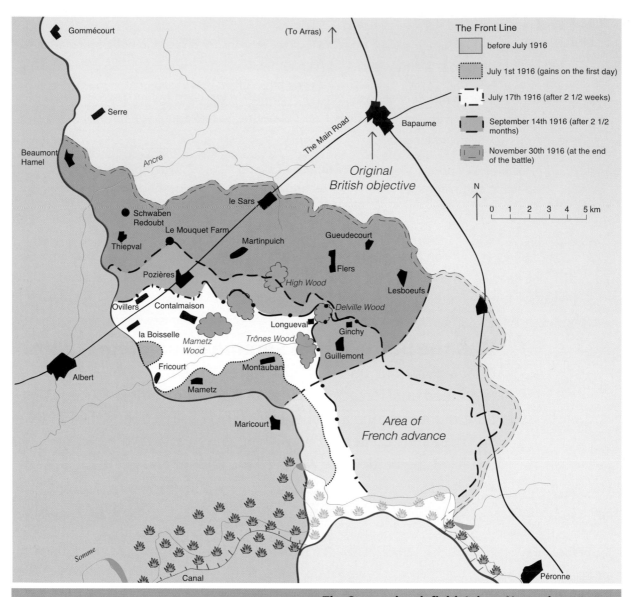

The front line:
- before July 1916
- July 1st 1916 (gains on the first day)
- July 17th 1916 (after 2 1/2 weeks)
- September 14th 1916 (after 2 1/2 months)
- November 30th 1916 (at the end of the battle)

The Somme battlefield, July to November 1916.

SOURCE K

We are slowly but surely killing off the best of the male population of these islands. Can we afford to go on paying the same sort of price for the same sort of gain?

A letter written by the politician Lord Lansdowne to the *Daily Telegraph*, 29 November 1916.

Key words

Infantry Soldiers that fight on foot.

SOURCE L

The scale and intensity of the British attack on 1 July 1916 had an immediate effect on the Germans, causing the transfer of 60 heavy guns and two **infantry** divisions from Verdun to the Somme, and an end to the German search for victory at Verdun.

A modern historian writing in 1994.

TASKS...

1 Study the map on page 178 and Sources G to L. They all provide some idea about whether the Battle of the Somme was a success or a failure.

   a) In your book, copy and complete the success/failure line below. Select what you think is the important point from the map and Sources G to L. Note these points in your own words in the appropriate place along the line. Where you position each point depends on how strongly you think it proves the Battle of the Somme was a success or a failure.

   Success ◄──────────────────────────────────► **Failure**

   b) Discuss your ideas with a partner to see if you agree on where each point should be placed.

2 Use the findings from the success/failure line to write a paragraph summarising your answer to the question: '*Was the Battle of the Somme a complete failure?*'

3 Copy the following comparison chart. Use the knowledge you have gained so far to fill in information about the different aspects of the Battle of the Somme. Later, you will need to add more information, so be sure to leave plenty of room for this. **ws**

Conflict	Main weapons	Tactics used	Scale of conflict	Who won?
First World War: Battle of the Somme				

SOURCE Ⓜ

A painting of the East Surrey Regiment kicking a football across No Man's Land, July 1916. Taken from the Illustrated London News, 29 July 1916.

Plenary

Take a look at Source M. This picture was shown to the British public as an image of the Battle of the Somme.

💡 How well do you feel Source M represents the battle?

💡 Why do you think the government would want to show images like this to the British public?

WHY DID FRANCE FALL IN 1940?

In this section you will find out:

- why the German army conquered France so easily in 1940
- how far weapons and tactics had changed by 1940
- whether Dunkirk was a German victory.

To investigate these ideas you will:

- create a plan of attack
- study the use of propaganda.

Starter

Look at the following map, which shows the position of French and British troops and possible places for a German invasion of France.

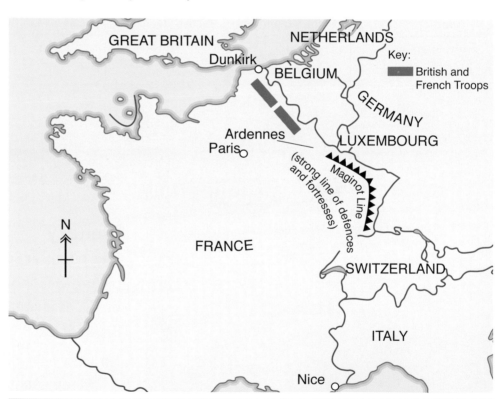

A map showing the position of British and French troops in 1940.

If you were a German commander, how would you plan an attack on France?

Using the map above, work in pairs to devise an invasion plan. Then share it with others in your class.

How did the Germans trick the Allied Forces?

In 1930 the French began building the Maginot Line (see the map below). They were determined not to let the Germans invade them again and suffer a similar experience to the First World War.

The Maginot Line was a series of strong **fortresses** about 145 kilometres long. It stretched along the French–German border as far as the Ardennes Forest. The French believed that the Maginot Line was invincible and couldn't be penetrated by attacking forces. They also believed it was impossible for the German army to move tanks and equipment through the dense Ardennes Forest and attack them there. Because of this, the French and the British concentrated their troops along the French–Belgian border, anticipating that a German attack would be launched from there, which is what had happened at the start of the First World War.

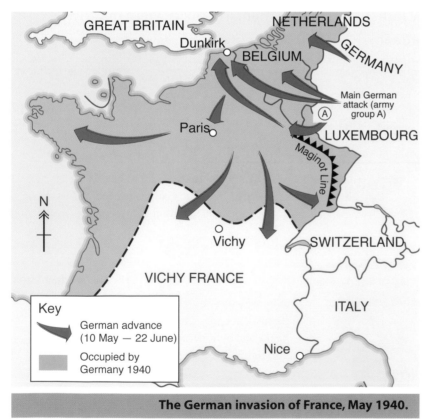

The German invasion of France, May 1940.

However the French were wrong. On 10 May 1940 the German army *did* launch an attack through Belgium and Holland, and the Allied Forces quickly sent their troops to deal with it. However, this attack was designed to draw attention *away* from the main German attack, led by army group A (see the map), which made its way quite easily through the Ardennes Forest. It was here that the real invasion of France began.

💡 Look back at the plan of attack which you drew for the Starter activity on page 180. How does it compare with the plan above, drawn by a real German commander?

How did the Germans conquer France so easily?

The German army began its advance into France on 10 May 1940. Three weeks later, British troops had been forced out of the country and, by the 22 June 1940, the conquest of France was complete. The main reason for this success was the German tactic know as *Blitzkrieg* (lightning war). This relied on three main features:

- speed of attack
- the element of surprise
- effective communication.

The Germans created Panzer divisions in order to make Blitzkrieg more effective (see below).

The Allies were slow to react to the *Blitzkrieg*. Counter-attacks were attempted but were disorganised and failed. British tanks were slow and poorly armed. They were still being used to support the infantry rather than to *lead* them. The Allies were quickly forced to retreat.

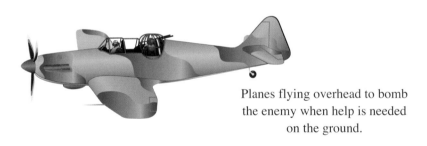

Planes flying overhead to bomb the enemy when help is needed on the ground.

Fast-moving scouts on motorbikes to find the enemy positions.

Tanks to destroy enemy tanks and positions, so that the rest of the army can follow.

Infantry in lorries so that they can keep up with the tanks and help when the fighting is fierce.

The Commander leads his men using the radio to communicate with them all.

German Panzer divisions. The idea behind a Panzer division was that planes, tanks, infantry and artillery could all work together to defeat the enemy. This was made possible by the radio which allowed the commander to control the different weapons.

SOURCE A

The tank engine is your weapon as much as its gun.

Spoken by Field Marshall Guderian, the creator and leader of Germany's Panzer divisions.

SOURCE B

Blitzkrieg could not exist without very close co-operation from all arms – that is, planes, tanks, infantry and artillery. In this respect, radiotelephony – the use of the radio to communicate – was the crucial element of this new style of war.

A modern historian writing about Blitzkrieg.

TASKS...

1 Take a look at Source A. What do you think Guderian meant when he said this?

2 Using all the information and sources on pages 182-3, write a 50-word summary that explains why the *Blitzkrieg* was so effective. You must write your explanation so that a Year 6 student can understand it.

Was the evacuation of Dunkirk a German victory?

By 27 May 1940 the Allied Forces had retreated to the channel port of Dunkirk on the French coast and were surrounded by the German army, which was closing in on them. A huge rescue attempt was mounted from Britain to bring the British troops safely home. However, while they were waiting on the beaches to be rescued, the German *Luftwaffe* (air force) bombed them.

TASKS...

1 Take a look at the two accounts below. This is how events at Dunkirk might have been portrayed in both the British and the German newspapers at the time.

What do you think the newspaper articles agree on?

Unbeatable! – thousands of British troops safely home

Under a barrage of enemy fire, ships of all sizes have bravely brought our troops back to England from Dunkirk. Many heroes have helped to create this miracle, bringing their little boats from far and wide to sail alongside our great navy to bring our army home. The men have returned gloriously and in high spirits, raring to go back soon and beat the Germans once and for all.

Victory! – British army pushed off French soil

What was once considered one of the most powerful armies in the world has been forced to flee from Dunkirk. The sheer power and speed of our advance completely overwhelmed the Allied Forces. Our magnificent *Luftwaffe* has made the evacuation miserable for them. In their hurry to escape, the British Army left most of their equipment and many prisoners. Our conquest of France is complete.

TASKS...

2 Both of the newspaper articles in task 1 are examples of propaganda and claim victory for their own side. Pick out three words or phrases from each article that have been used deliberately to persuade you that they were the victors. Put the words in a chart like the one below. Two examples have been done for you. Do not fill in the 'Neutral' column just yet.

British propaganda	Neutral	German propaganda
Unbeatable		*Victory*

3 Look at the statements below, which each contain facts about Dunkirk. Which of these statements do you think support the British account and which support the German account? Add them to your chart above by writing down the number of each fact in the correct place. Some facts do not support either viewpoint. Add these numbers to the neutral column.

1 Nearly 340,000 British and Allied troops were successfully evacuated between 27 May and 4 June 1940. The government had hoped to rescue about 50,000.

2 After Dunkirk, the Germans had to turn south and capture the remaining parts of France, particularly Paris. On 22 June 1940, about three weeks after Dunkirk, the French signed an armistice (peace agreement) with Adolf Hitler to mark their surrender.

3 In the evacuation, the British left behind most of their heavy military equipment, comprising 75,000 vehicles (including 475 tanks), 2500 anti-aircraft guns and 11,000 machine-guns. These fell into the hands of the Germans.

4 The *Luftwaffe's* bombing of the beaches was not very successful because the sand absorbed the explosive shock and casualties were few.

5 The Royal Navy worked hard, risking its ships (which were in short supply) and the lives of crew members to get men aboard as calmly as possible. Eyewitnesses praised them for this.

6 More than 68,000 British soldiers were killed, wounded, captured or missing.

8 By saving the British Expeditionary Force (BEF), the British government had kept its professional army alive. It would be able to fight in future campaigns and train new recruits.

7 The Royal Air Force (RAF) did little to support the evacuation of Dunkirk, allowing the *Luftwaffe* to bomb the ships and beaches. The RAF was later heavily criticised for this by Dunkirk survivors.

9 Only 26,500 of the 340,000 troops were rescued by civilian boats.

4   Use the information on your chart to write a balanced and unbiased newspaper report about what happened at Dunkirk. Your aim is to give a truthful account of events and reach a realistic judgement about whose victory it was. You must support the points you make with evidence.

- Think of a headline that tells people about the key event. Your headline should be no more than six words long.

- In your report you need to concentrate on the facts about what happened using the statements in your chart. You will need to use connectives to sequence and report the events in order that they happened: *firstly, secondly, meanwhile, later, because, next, however, although*.

- As well as writing about the evacuation of Dunkirk itself, you will need to describe the background to it to explain why it was necessary.

- Finally, you need to end your report with your judgement on whose victory Dunkirk really was. You should write about why the British and the Germans would each consider it a victory and what *you* think about victory.

- Try to make your judgement balanced and use evidence to back up what you say. Use connectives to offer your judgement: *on the one hand, on the other hand, on balance*.

- Then use connectives to back up your judgement: *this shows that, as in, this is suggested by*.

- Remember, as this is a newspaper article it may be partly written in the present tense. You may also wish to include eyewitness interviews.

- Make sure that you show all sides of what happened and do not use biased language.

Plenary

Look back to your comparison chart, which you began on page 179.

Add a second row about the fall of France in the Second World War (as below), then fill in the details. **WS**

Conflict	Main weapons	Tactics used	Scale of conflict	Who won?
First World War: Battle of the Somme				
Second World War: the fall of France				

This chart is still not complete, so make sure there is enough space for one more comparison, which will come at the end of the chapter.

WHAT HAPPENED DURING THE CUBAN MISSILE CRISIS?

Objectives

In this section you will find out:

- how close the USA and Soviet Union came to nuclear war in 1962
- who 'won' the Cuban Missile Crisis.

To investigate these ideas you will:

- analyse sources
- interpret a timeline to write a diary.

Starter

Study the map below, then answer the questions that follow.

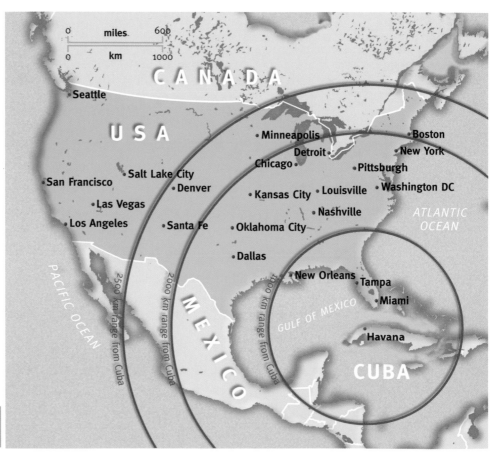

The location of the USA and Cuba.

💡 *What do you think this map is showing?*

💡 *Think of three questions you would like to ask to find out more. Write these questions down.*

What was the Cold War about?

After the Second World War the United States and the Soviet Union, who had worked together to defeat Hitler, grew suspicious of each other. The main reason for this was that the Soviet Union was a communist country and the US was a capitalist country (see pages 164–5). They had different beliefs about how a country should be run and how people should live their lives. They each thought their way was the best and saw the other way as a threat. This period of rivalry and suspicion was known as the Cold War – a war of words, threats and propaganda.

💡 Are there any new questions you would now like to ask about the map on page 186? Write these down.

Nuclear weapons

The distrust and rivalry between the Soviet Union and the USA grew even stronger in 1949, when the USSR developed a nuclear bomb. (The USA had used nuclear bombs against Japan in 1945.) The two countries began to compete to develop more powerful nuclear weapons which could be fired over a longer-range (see page 168). By the 1960s, both countries had enough nuclear weapons to destroy the world several times over.

💡 Are there any new questions you would like to ask about the map on page 186? Write these down.

The significance of Cuba

Cuba is a small island about 145 kilometres from the southern tip of the USA. In 1959 it became a communist state and began to trade with the Soviet Union. Nikita Khrushchev, the Soviet President, was pleased to have an alliance with a country so close to the USA, especially as the USA had built missile launch sites on the Turkish–Soviet border with Turkey's permission. The Turkish launch sites enabled an American nuclear missile to reach Moscow in five to ten minutes, so the Soviet President saw them as a huge threat.

💡 Does this additional information help you to answer any of your questions from page 186? Use it to try to explain what you now think the map on page 186 shows. Share your thoughts with the class.

What happened during the Cuban Missile Crisis?

The Cuban Missile Crisis was the most serious crisis in the Cold War period. It almost caused a nuclear war between the USA and the Soviet Union. People around the world were very frightened as mass destruction was a real possibility. The timeline below shows how the crisis developed and how it was resolved.

TIMELINE
The Cuban Missile Crisis, October 1962

Tuesday 16 — Nuclear missile launch sites are photographed on Cuba by US spy planes. Experts say they could hit most US cities within seventeen minutes and would be ready to launch in seven days. At the same time, twenty ships from the Soviet Union are spotted heading towards Cuba. The ships are carrying nuclear missiles. The US President, John F. Kennedy, has to decide what to do – taking into account that there may already be nuclear missiles on Cuba.

Monday 22 — President Kennedy uses his navy to blockade (surround) Cuba to prevent the Soviet ships from getting through.

Tuesday 23 — President Khrushchev threatens that his ships will force their way through the US blockade if necessary. This would be an act of war.

Wednesday 24 — The first Soviet ships approach the 800-kilometre blockade zone. It appears that they will force their way through the blockade but, at 10.32 am, they stop and turn round.

Thursday 25 — Some of President Kennedy's advisers recommend an invasion of Cuba to destroy the remaining missiles. This would be an act of war, which Kennedy wants to avoid.

Friday 26 — Khrushchev says he will remove the missiles if Kennedy lifts the blockade and promises not to invade Cuba.

Saturday 27 — Kennedy's advisers still want the US to invade Cuba, despite Khrushchev's offer.

Sunday 28 — Kennedy accepts Khrushchev's offer. He also makes a secret agreement to remove US missiles from Turkey. Khrushchev agrees to begin removing missiles from Cuba. The Cuban Missile Crisis is over.

A cartoon about the Cuban Missile Crisis, published in 1962. Kennedy is on the right, Khrushchev is on the left.

TASKS...

1 **ws** **a)** On a large piece of paper draw the outline of a diary with each date on the timeline marked on it. Use the timeline on page 188 to help you.

Notice the clockface in the top corner of the diary on the right. This represents the Nuclear Clock, which was designed by the US magazine *Bulletin* in 1947 as a symbol of nuclear danger. The original design was set at seven minutes to midnight, and minutes were taken off or added on depending how close nuclear war was thought to be.

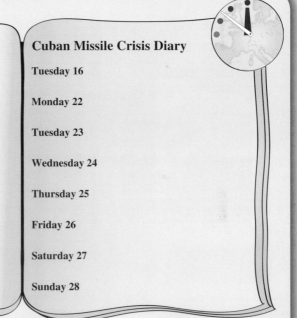

Cuban Missile Crisis Diary

Tuesday 16

Monday 22

Tuesday 23

Wednesday 24

Thursday 25

Friday 26

Saturday 27

Sunday 28

b) Complete the diary for each day of the Cuban Missile Crisis using the timeline on page 188 and the instructions below.

- You must decide each day how many minutes should be added on or taken off your nuclear clock. From that, you should work out what time it would be on each day.

- You may add or take off up to three minutes each day, depending on how important you feel the events of each day are. If you think there is no change on one day, you may leave the clock on the time it was on the previous day.

- Remember, if the clock reaches midnight then war has broken out.

- In each diary entry, you must explain how the clock time has changed and why you have changed it. If you have added two minutes instead of one or three in relation to the event that has taken place, explain why.

- You should also say how you would be feeling on each day as the crisis develops.

2 Look carefully at your completed diary. On which day were you closest to midnight? Explain why.

3 What time was it on your clock at the end of the Cuban Missile Crisis? What do you think this suggests about the way the crisis was resolved?

4 By 1963 the Nuclear Clock was set at twelve minutes to midnight. What does this suggest about relations between the USA and the Soviet Union after the Cuban Missile Crisis? Why do you think this was? Discuss your answers with the rest of the class.

Who 'won' the Cuban Missile Crisis?

Even though there had been no fighting, both the USA and the Soviet Union claimed victory in the Cuban Missile Crisis. Look at what President Kennedy and President Khrushchev said about the end of the Cuban Missile Crisis.

I have proved that I can stand up to the communist Soviet Union and force it to back down without causing a war. The USA is no longer under threat of direct nuclear attack from Cuba because of my firm but sensible approach.

President Kennedy.

I have prevented nuclear war by my power of compromise. The Americans have gained nothing. Cuba is still communist and Kennedy has promised to remove his missiles from Turkey (though he will not admit this publicly).

President Khrushchev.

SOURCE **B**

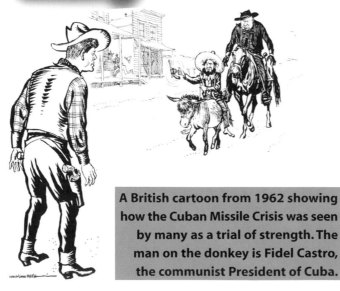

A British cartoon from 1962 showing how the Cuban Missile Crisis was seen by many as a trial of strength. The man on the donkey is Fidel Castro, the communist President of Cuba.

The Cold War was a war of propaganda as well as threats. Many cartoons like the one shown in Source B were published about the Cuban Missile Crisis, each giving its own interpretation of events.

TASKS...

1 **WS** In pairs, produce two political cartoons about the outcome of the Cuban Missile Crisis. One of you will design a cartoon to illustrate the US point of view about who 'won', the other will design a cartoon to illustrate the Soviet point of view. Think carefully about the words and pictures you will use in your cartoon to get your message across and to persuade people that your side is the victorious one.

2 Compare your cartoon with your partner's. Then show it to others in your class, explaining how you have tried to get your message across.

3 Look back at your comparison chart, which you started on page 179 and added to on page 185. Add a third row about the Cuban Missile Crisis (as shown below) and complete the details of each aspect of warfare.

Conflict	Main weapons	Tactics used	Scale of conflict	Who won?
First World War: Battle of the Somme				
Second World War: the fall of France				
Cold war: the Cuban Missile Crisis				

EXTENSION TASK...

4 Use all of the information on your comparison chart and the text in this chapter to write an essay entitled: '*How and why did warfare change in the twentieth century?*' **WS**

Plenary

Having studied the Battle of the Somme during the First World War, the fall of France during the Second World War and the Cuban Missile Crisis during the Cold War, which aspect of warfare do you think has changed:

a) the most   b) the least?

Discuss this with a partner and the rest of the class. How far do you agree with each other?

💡 How accurate can our judgements of changing warfare be after studying just three events from the twentieth century?

HOW HAVE ATTITUDES TOWARDS RECRUITMENT CHANGED?

Objectives

In this section you will find out:
- about changing attitudes towards recruitment during the First World War, the Second World War and the Vietnam War.

To investigate these ideas you will:
- study different propaganda posters
- show examples of attitudes towards recruitment during each war.

Starter

Look at Sources A, B and C. Then answer the questions on page 193.

SOURCE A

A recruitment poster produced by the British government in 1915.

SOURCE B

"Let 'em all come"

MEN 41-55

HOME DEFENCE BATTALIONS
Apply at any Army Recruiting Centre Now

A recruitment poster from the Second World War.

SOURCE C

I WANT OUT

An American anti-war poster from the Vietnam War.

💡 Who do each of the posters on page 192 appeal to?

💡 What methods do they use to attract attention?

💡 What impressions do they give of warfare?

💡 Which poster is the odd one out? Why?

What happened at the start of the First World War?

When war was declared in 1914, people throughout Britain and Europe were very enthusiastic about the glory and drama of fighting. In Britain, **war fever** spread quickly. Thousands of people were singing and dancing in the streets, keen to show how **patriotic** they were and how much they hated the Germans.

> ### Key words
>
> **War fever** Enthusiasm for the war.
>
> **Patriotic** Loyal to one's country.
>
> **Enlist** Join the armed forces.

A young working-class recruit in 1914.

> *What a chance for a great adventure, a way of escaping working-class areas and the chance to travel to new places.*

> *The war will be over by Christmas.*

> *My friends are all joining up and fighting for king and country. I don't want to miss out on this experience.*

> *Our town has to have more men fighting than the one next to us*

> *It's about pride! I can't let everyone down.*

> *If I join up with my friends, at least we will all be fighting together.*

Although most men were very enthusiastic at the outbreak of the First World War, some men had doubts. So the British government, led by Lord Kitchener, introduced a huge propaganda campaign, distributing posters and leaflets throughout the country. This campaign was very successful. More than half a million men **enlisted** by the end of the first month of the war, and two million signed up by 1916.

Why did the government introduce conscription in 1916?

In 1914 there had been an initial rush of men wanting to join up. However by 1916 there was a shortage of recruits. To overcome this problem the government introduced conscription. All single men between the ages of eighteen and 40 had to 'join up'. In March 1916 conscription was changed to include all married men.

Conscientious objectors

Some men refused to be conscripted into the army. These men became known as conscientious objectors, or conchies. They were very unpopular and labelled as cowards by the British public. Many of them were called up in front of Military Tribunal Officers and had to explain their reasons for not wanting to fight.

> *To force people to fight is wrong. Conscription is taking away people's freedom. This is a war between governments, not people.*

> *I am patriotic, but as a pacifist, I believe that war is wrong. I refuse to kill other human beings.*

> *I am a religious Quaker, I do not believe in violence.*

> *My job is vital to the war effort. It would be impossible for me to leave it. Nothing can be gained from this war. It is wrong.*

> *I am of poor sight and poor health. I will be of no use in the army.*

TASKS...

1. Look at the reasons the man gives on page 193 for wanting to fight. Which reason do you think would appeal to most men? Explain you answer.

2. Look at the reasons the conscientious objectors gave for not wanting to fight.

   a) What reasons might the Military Tribunal Officers be sympathetic towards? Explain your decision.

   b) What reasons would they be less sympathetic towards? Why?

3. Look back at Source A on page 192, which shows a propaganda poster that the British government used during the First World War.

   a) What comments do you think a conscientious objector might make in relation to this?

   b) What changes do you think conscientious objectors might make to this poster in order to support their beliefs?

4. In your book, draw an arrow like the one below. Give examples of six words that you think people would have most and least commonly used at the outbreak of the First World War. (There are some examples below that you can use.)

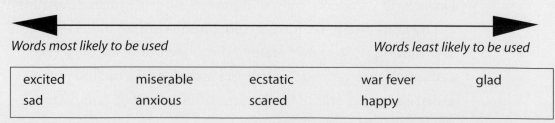

Words most likely to be used — Words least likely to be used

excited	miserable	ecstatic	war fever	glad
sad	anxious	scared	happy	

MODERN TIMES 1750–1990

194

What happened during the Second World War?

Britain entered the Second World War on 3 September 1939, when it declared war on Germany. All men aged between eighteen and forty were conscripted into the British army. Only coal miners, firemen and doctors were **exempt**.

- 💡 *Why do you think that conscription was introduced as soon as war was declared?*

- 💡 *What does this suggest that the government had learned from the First World War?*

- 💡 *Why do you think the three groups of men mentioned above were exempt?*

- 💡 *What arguments could you make for and against their exemption?*

WOMEN OF BRITAIN
COME INTO
THE FACTORIES
ASK AT ANY EMPLOYMENT EXCHANGE FOR ADVICE AND FULL DETAILS

A poster from the Second World War advertising for women to help the war effort by working in factories.

Key words

Exempt Free from duty.

Home front The contribution of civilians to the war effort.

How had conscription changed since the First World War?

As with the First World War, there was initial enthusiasm for the Second World War. However, the idea of war was no longer new or exciting because people were too aware of the death and destruction it caused.

As men were conscripted into the army, the government had to adopt a different approach to keep public support. They immediately issued the Emergency Powers Defence Act, which gave the government total control over the whole of the British population. The Act allowed the government to direct people in any way that they wanted. The government could also confiscate property for the benefit of the state. There was also a huge propaganda campaign encouraging civilians to help.

Conscription was much fairer during the Second World War because all eligible men, regardless of class, were expected to join up. Between April 1939 and 1940 more than one million men joined up. The civilian response to the government's request for help on the **home front** was also positive.

"Let 'em all come"

MEN 41-55

HOME DEFENCE BATTALIONS

Apply at any Army Recruiting Centre Now

A poster encouraging men to volunteer for the Home Guard. The Home Guard consisted of unpaid part-time volunteers who were too old for military service. They were trained to defend Britain against invasion.

SOURCE F

The whole of the warring nations are engaged, not only soldiers, but the entire population – men, women and children. The fronts are everywhere. The trenches are dug in towns and streets. Every village is fortified. Every road is barred. The front lines run through the factories. The workmen are soldiers with different weapons, but the same courage.

Spoken by Winston Churchill, the British prime minister, in 1940.

TASKS...

1 Look at Source F. How do you think Churchill is encouraging people to join the war effort?

2 Which different groups of people is Churchill appealing to?

3 Look at the information on pages 195–6 and Sources D to F. In pairs, note down all the changes in methods of recruitment since the First World War.

4 Do you think the changes in methods of recruitment during the Second World War were needed? Give reasons for your answer.

5 In your book draw another arrow similar to task 4 on page 194. Give examples of six words that you think people would have used most and least commonly at the outbreak of the Second World War.

THE VIETNAM WAR

Look in an atlas to find out where Vietnam is.

factfile

At the end of the Second World War, the USA became involved in a Cold War against the USSR. The two superpowers had opposing ideologies and both felt very threatened by the other.

The USA believed that as a democratic country it was their duty to protect others from communism. At first the USA became involved in Vietnam because they wanted to contain communism. The Americans believed that if Vietnam became a communist country it would have a domino effect on the rest of Indochina.

When the USA first became involved in the Vietnam War in the 1950s and 1960s the majority of the American people supported their government's actions. However, between 1964 and 1970 the American role in Vietnam changed drastically.

- There seemed to be no quick victory in sight.
- The Vietnamese were using guerrilla tactics, which the American army found very difficult to fight against and defeat.
- To try to combat this problem, the Americans sent more and more men to fight. By 1969, there were over half a million troops in Vietnam and more were still needed.

As the war continued, people lost their patience with and confidence in the government. They wanted the war to end and their young men to return home safely. Many took drastic measures to force their government to end the war.

TASKS...

Look at the spider diagram on page 198. Using the spider diagram and the information on this page, answer the following questions.

1 Why did so many people object to the war in Vietnam?

2 Which of the different groups that opposed the Vietnam War do you think had the greatest impact on public opinion? Give reasons for your answer.

3 Draw an arrow like the one on page 194. Give examples of 6 words, which you think that people would have used most and least commonly during the Vietnam War.

'No' say the general public

The American public quickly became disillusioned with the government's involvement in Vietnam. People were watching atrocities being committed by their young soldiers, hearing about the widespread problem of drug abuse and, worst of all, they were seeing many of their young men return home in body bags.

'No' say the war veterans

Many war veterans also campaigned for the war to be ended. Often badly injured, in wheelchairs or disfigured, they would give speeches about what was happening in Vietnam. On occasions they threw their medals into the crowds.

YOU WILL FIGHT!

'No' say civil rights campaigners

The draft led to problems within the USA. Many educated white Americans found legitimate ways of avoiding the draft. Poorer Americans, many of whom were black, did the majority of the fighting. This led to civil rights activists like Martin Luther King joining the anti-war movement.

'No' say the students

Thousands of young men burnt their draft cards in public places, some refused to turn up for training, others fled to Canada or Europe in order to avoid the draft. In May 1968, there were reports of people in Cantonsville, Maryland, breaking into the draft board offices and destroying records. By 1969, there were over 34,000 draft dodgers.

'Yes' say a minority

There were still some people who supported the war. They saw themselves as patriotic. They also held demonstrations in favour of the war to show their support for President Johnson's policy in Vietnam.

Plenary

Look back at the three word arrows you have drawn in this section. How have the words changed? Why do you think they have changed?

In March 2003, thousands of people took to the streets in mass demonstrations across the world in order to show their disapproval of the war against Iraq. Why do you think that so many people in the twenty-first century disapprove of war? Are any of the reasons similar to those from the First World War, Second World War or the Vietnam War?

Do you think that a government should have the right to force civilians to fight for their country during a war that it is involved in?

EVERYDAY LIFE: WHAT IMPACT DOES WARFARE HAVE ON CIVILIANS?

Objectives

In this section you will find out:
- how the impact of warfare on civilian life varied greatly during the First and Second World Wars and the Vietnam War
- how the government introduced laws to influence civilians' everyday lives
- about the differences between short-term and long-term effects of warfare on civilian lives.

To investigate these ideas you will:
- categorise the ways in which civilians were affected.

Starter

If a foreign power invaded your country tomorrow, how would you feel? How would your everyday life be affected?

How would you resist?

Write down your ideas for each question and share them with the rest of the class.

What were civilians' experiences during the First World War?

Read the conversation between Doris and Joan on the next page, then study Sources A, B and C on page 201.

A conversation between Doris and Joan in 1918

Oh, Doris! Can you believe, how much our lives have changed since war was declared in 1914?

I know. War fever spread throughout the country. Well, that was over three years ago and there's no end to the war in sight.

All the male members of our families have gone off to fight. Just thinking about those who have died makes me really sad and angry. Even John, at the age of 45, was conscripted into the army when the volunteers ran out.

I still can't believe how much control the government has over our lives since the Defence of the Realm Act (DORA) was introduced in 1914.

I know. We don't even know much about what's happening because the government censors any news or information that we receive via letters or in the newspapers.

I can't remember the last time I went flying kites with the children, saw any bonfires or fireworks being lit, or even heard the local church bells ring.

The government have taken control of the nearby fields to grow crops on. You're not even allowed to walk through the allotments or by the railway lines any more.

We shouldn't really complain though. At least our lives are not at risk. We hardly see any Zeppelin air raids here. We have just about enough food to keep us going.

Well, that's only because the government is encouraging us to grow our own food because the German submarines have been sinking our supply ships. They have also introduced rationing, which means that everybody is guaranteed a small amount of sugar, margarine and meat. Some people are eating better than before the war started!

The older men complain that they no longer have a social life and don't enjoy drinking, because the beer is watered down.

Oh well. Haven't got time to stand around talking all day. Must get ready for work and be off to the munitions factory to start my shift.

At least when the war is over our lives can get back to normal!

In August 1914 the government passed the Defence of the Realm Act (DORA). It gave the government greater power over people's lives than ever before. People could be told where to work. Railways and coal mines were taken over by the government because they were essential to the war effort. British Summer Time was introduced: clocks went forward an hour to provide more daylight working hours. In 1916 bank holidays were cancelled. So was Bonfire Night.

DORA affected people's lives in many other ways too. Pub opening hours were cut and the beer was watered down. It was forbidden to buy someone else a drink or to feed bread to an animal. DORA even restricted the kind of kite you could fly.

DORA gave the government control over all the newspapers. Newspapers were not allowed to tell the truth about the conditions on the Western Front.

A modern historian describes the effects of DORA.

SOURCE **B**

A government poster of 1917.

SOURCE **C**

A government poster of 1917 encouraging women to join the Women's Land Army.

💡 In what ways do Sources A, B and C support Doris and Joan's conversation?

💡 Which source is the most useful to an historian who wants to find out about changes to civilians' lives during the First World War? Give reasons for your answer.

TASKS...

1 Look at the conversation between Doris and Joan, and Sources A, B and C.

   a) Copy and complete columns 1 and 2 in the chart below. For each change say why you think it was introduced. (You should give at least seven changes.)

Change introduced by DORA	Why it was introduced	Impact on civilian lives (number 1–5)	Reason for decision

   b) Decide how much impact each change would have had on peoples' lives in column 3. (Put a 1 if it had a minor impact and a 5 if it had a major impact.) Write down the reasons for your decision in the fourth column.

   c) Shade the changes that were made to protect civilians in one colour, and the changes that were introduced to protect the soldiers in another colour.

2 How great an impact did the First World War have on the everyday lives of civilians? Discuss your ideas with a partner.

3 What other information would you need to help you find out about the full impact of the First World War on civilians' everyday lives?

How did life change for civilians during the Second World War?

- Collection bins were used to gather paper and metal so they could be used in the war effort. Paper could be recycled, bones provided cartridges for guns, aluminium pans and iron railings were used for Spitfire planes.

- Street names and signposts were taken down – if the country was invaded, this would lead to confusion.

- Gas masks were issued to everyone at the outbreak of war.

- Plans were also made to evacuate children from the towns to the countryside where they would be safer.

- Each family was issued with ration books in January 1940. They could only buy limited amounts of meat, sugar, tea, coffee and tobacco. You were only allowed to use your ration coupons at one shop.

- As the sinking of supply ships led to food shortages among the British population, people were encouraged to grow their own food.

- Home-grown fruit, vegetables and bread were not rationed. As a result, many people began to grow fruit and vegetables in their gardens and allotments. People also kept hens and geese.

A public information leaflet telling people what to do to protect themselves against gas attacks.

A 'Make Do and Mend' campaign was introduced by the government. Old woollen clothing was unpicked by volunteers and re-knitted into warm clothing for the British troops. Nylon parachute material was sold for underwear. Sheets were patched or turned into bandages. Envelopes were re-used and newspapers were recycled. Even scrap food was collected in bins on street corners and taken to farms to feed the pigs.

A modern historian writing in 2002.

A pamphlet supplied by the Ministry of Food in 1941, describing how to use rations effectively.

Milk	6 glasses
Eggs	1 per fortnight
Meat	500 grams
Butter or margarine	300 grams
Sugar	2 teacups
Cooking oil	$\frac{1}{2}$ a teacup
Tea	just under 1 teacup of dry tea leaves
Cheese	225 grams
Jam	$1\frac{1}{2}$ teacups

Average weekly adult ration during wartime.

SOURCE H

The Ministry of Information was responsible for the poster campaigns which encouraged people to join the voluntary services and to work hard and save in order to help the war effort. It also produced posters which warned people of the dangers of 'careless talk'. There was a fear that German spies could be working in the country so people were told not to discuss the war in public.

From a modern textbook.

SOURCE I

Fishermen on Holy Island, off the north-east coast of England, learning to use rifles as part of their Home Guard training.

- The Home Guard was set up to help defend the country against invasion. The men in the Home Guard were either too young, too old or too unfit to fight. They included First World War veterans.

- Anderson Shelters were built in houses with gardens. These were made from steel sheets and buried 4 feet (about 1.2 metres) deep.

- Blackout curtains were used in order to prevent any light escaping from houses during the night – light could have been seen by enemy bomber planes.

TASKS...

1   Read the information and Sources D to I on pages 202–4.

   a) Copy the mind map below into your books.

> *Changes to protect the population during an air raid.*

> *Changes to protect the population in the event of an invasion.*

> **Examples of changes that were made on the home front during the Second World War.**

> *Changes that contribute to the war effort and make life easier.*

   b) Add as many examples as possible to show each type of change.

TASKS...

2 Look back to the conversation between Doris and Joan on page 200. How would their lives have changed during the Second World War?

a) With a partner, re-write the conversation between Doris and Joan as it might take place in 1944.

b) Make sure you explain why the different changes have been introduced.

3 What similarities and differences can you see between the lives of civilians in the First and Second World Wars? Discuss your answer with a partner.

Case study: how did the Blitz affect life in Britain?

During the Second World War, both the German and British governments believed it was important to bomb industrial, military and communications targets. It was accepted that civilians would also be targeted, injured and killed. Both governments thought that if civilians were hit hard it may lead to the war ending more quickly. Governments thought that people would be frightened, morale would get worse and that people would question what their governments were doing. (This is what had happened during the First World War when naval blockades had meant that thousands faced starvation and German civilians had begged the government to surrender.) The British and German governments hoped that during the Second World War bombing campaigns civilians might pressurise their government to surrender, bringing an end to the war.

 SOURCE J

 SOURCE K

7 October 1940	We must continue to attack England on all fronts.
11 October 1940	We shall be able to force England to its knees during the next few weeks.
12 October 1940	Horrific reports from London. A metropolis on the slide. An international drama without parallel, but we must see it through.
23 October 1940	We shall battle on to destroy their last hope.
1 November 1940	The Führer intends to keep hammering the English until they break.

Extracts from the diary of Joseph Goebbels, a senior Nazi, describing intense bombing raids on Britain.

We will make the enemy burn and bleed in every way.

A quote from Winston Churchill in 1941.

💡 Look at Sources J and K. What reasons do Goebbels and Churchill give for the importance of bombing during the Second World War?

Coventry Cathedral in ruins after a night of heavy bombing during the Blitz, November 1940. The city centre was destroyed and over 500 people were killed.

What happened in the Blitz?

Between autumn 1940 and May 1941, the German government launched major bombing raids on London, Coventry, Manchester, and many other industrial and coastal areas. German bombs destroyed some of the oldest buildings in the country.

These attacks became known as the Blitz. Thousands of houses were destroyed and thousands of civilians were injured and killed – despite the warnings given by air raid sirens and the protection of bomb shelters (see Source P).

The British government gave everyone gas masks and arranged for children to be evacuated to the countryside, where it was supposedly safer. Nevertheless, casualty rates during the Blitz were huge.

When the Blitz ended in May 1941, more than 43,000 people across Britain had been killed. Many more had been left homeless. Half-way through the Second World War, there had been more women and children killed than soldiers.

SOURCE Ⓜ

SOURCE Ⓝ

Children from London evacuated to the Sussex coast, awaiting transport to their new homes, July 1940.

Schoolchildren	827,000
Mothers and children	524,000
Pregnant women	13,000
Blind and disabled people	7000
Teachers	103,000

Number of people evacuated in September 1939.

SOURCE O

The church was a popular shelter so it was full when the bomb fell. The bomb had burst in the middle of the shelterers, mostly women and small children. The scene resembled a massacre, with bodies, limbs, blood and flesh mingled with little hats, coats and shoes … The stench was the worst thing about it – that, and having to realise that these frightful pieces of flesh had once been living breathing people.

An account of the Blitz from a fireman, September 1940.

SOURCE P

People sleeping in a Morrison shelter, set up in their living room in London, September 1940.

SOURCE Q

Morrison shelters proved their worth over and over again. Countless families escaped uninjured, although their shelters were completely buried in debris. Police officers and rescue workers regularly report how people emerged smiling and safe from the wreckage of their homes.

From an Exeter newspaper in May 1942. Exeter was very badly hit by bombs during the war.

SOURCE R

SOURCE S

The whole story of the last weekend has been one of unplanned panic. The newspaper versions of life going on normally are grotesque. There was no bread, no milk and no telephones. There is no humour or laughter.

From a report by local officials on conditions in London, September 1940.

A photograph, posed for propaganda purposes, showing a milkman delivering among the ruins of a bombed city.

Extensive bomb damage in Walthamstow, London, September 1944.

TASKS...

1 a) Look at Sources L to T. Think of as many words as you can to describe how a British civilian might have felt during the Blitz. Write them down.

   b) Shade the positive words in one colour and the negative words in a second colour.

   c) Pair up and swap your selection of words with your partner.
   • How are the words that you chose similar? Explain why.
   • How are they different? Explain why.

2 Look at Sources L, M, P, R and T.

   a) Which pictures would a British newspaper be most likely to use?

   b) Which pictures would a German newspaper be most likely to use?

   c) Why might the British and German newspapers use different images?

   d) Create some headlines that might appear in either German or British newspapers to accompany the images.

3 What other information would you need in order to gain a balanced view of life during the Blitz?

What impact did warfare have on civilians during the Vietnam War?

The original napalm bomb wasn't so hot. If the **gooks** were quick, they could scrape it off. So the boys started adding polystyrene. Now it really sticks. But then if the gooks jumped into water, it stopped burning. So they started adding white phosphorous, to make it burn better. It'll burn under water now. One drop is enough. It'll keep burning right down to the bone, so they die from phosphorous poisoning.

A US pilot describes the effects of bombing with napalm.

Key words

Gooks A slang term that US soldiers used to refer to the Vietnamese.

The story below is based on real events from the Vietnam War.

At the time, I thought that I was lucky to survive. Many of my family, friends and fellow villagers died when the US and Vietcong soldiers raided and attacked our land. The sights that I saw were horrifying. People being shot at point blank range, women being raped for no reason, whole villages and crop fields being burned down.

Over four million Vietnamese people were killed during this war. Many others have died since from the man-made booby traps that have been left in our countryside and rice fields.

The US and Vietcong soldiers destroyed everything, especially our forests. Some 25,000 square kilometres were totally ruined.

The napalm bombs caused horrific burns and injuries. Many people were totally disfigured after these attacks and retreated into hiding because they were too scared to be seen in public.

Agent Orange was terrible, too. It totally destroyed the beautiful countryside and left huge scars on the land. Many of these are still seen today. People are now seen fishing in huge craters which were left by the B-52 bombers, the US planes that carried Agent Orange.

SOURCE V

Dead civilians, massacred at My Lai by US soldiers, 1968.

SOURCE W

Vietnamese children flee after a napalm attack , 1972.

Many Vietnamese suffered from sickness and headaches after Agent Orange attacks. More recently there have been widespread cases of cancer and birth defects in these areas, as the poison seeped into our water supplies.

I managed to flee from the North Vietnamese soldiers in 1975, as did thousands of other refugees. We had nowhere to go. But we had to escape because many dreadful things could have happened to us if we stayed.

Those who could not get away faced many problems. It was difficult to care for the orphans and the thousands of injured civilians and soldiers. There was widespread unemployment and starvation because the crop fields had been destroyed. The USA also imposed trade barriers, which made it impossible to buy and sell any goods.

After the war some people tried to leave Vietnam illegally by boat in order to live in a safe place. They became known as Boat People. Few survived. Either their boats were attacked by pirates who would steal their food, or they were refused entry by other countries who did not want to deal with the problem of refugees.

What a mess the Vietnam War left us all in!

TASKS...

1 **a)** According to Source U, what impact did the Vietnam War have on civilians' everyday lives?

   b) What other questions would you like to ask in order to find out more about the impact of the Vietnam War on civilians' lives? Use the '5Ws' strategy to help you.

2 Copy the diagram on the right into your books. You need to complete this diagram by giving examples of the following effects.

   a) The short-term effects of the Vietnam War on civilians' everyday lives.

   b) The long-term effects of the Vietnam War on civilians' everyday lives.

   Long-term effects

   Effects of the Vietnam War on everyday life.

   Short-term effects

3 What links can you make between the short-term and long-term effects of the Vietnam War on civilians' everyday lives? Draw arrows on your diagram to show these links and explain how they are linked.

4 How else could you categorise the effects of the Vietnam War on civilians?

Plenary

What similarities and differences can you see between the lives of civilians in the First and Second World Wars and the Vietnam War?

The impact of the Vietnam War on US civilians' everyday lives has not been included in this section. Do you think that it should have been? Explain your decision.

WHAT IMPACT HAS WAR HAD ON WOMEN'S LIVES?

In this section you will find out:
- why women's roles changed during the First and the Second World Wars
- what impact these changes had on the position of women in society.

To investigate these ideas you will:
- analyse the work that women did
- evaluate a variety of sources.

Starter

Our industries are suffering. We cannot provide enough munitions for our soldiers on the Western Front.

Urgent help is needed – not enough help is being given to injured soldiers on the battlefield.

Too many men are involved in clerical jobs. These are stopping them from fighting.

Not enough food is arriving in Britain. We may not be able to feed our people for much longer.

Life may become chaotic because there is no one to take over many of the jobs the men left behind.

Key words

Western Front The area of fighting in Belgium and France in the First World War.

💡 Which of the above problems do you think is most serious? Why?

💡 What suggestions would you make to help this government minister solve some of these problems?

What was the impact of the First World War on women?

With the outbreak of the First World War, 190,000 women lost their jobs. Most of the women who lost their jobs worked in the textiles industry and domestic services – with the outbreak of war, no one wanted to buy new clothes or rely on outside help with their families.

In 1915 the government had to produce more ammunition for soldiers on the Western Front. So it was agreed that women could have the men's jobs until they returned from war. But there was one condition: they would not receive the same pay as the men.

A Women's War Register was set up to find out which women were available for war work. The register had a positive response. In just over two weeks approximately 33,000 women signed up. In the following months this increased to more than 100,000 women.

By 1916, with the high number of men fighting abroad, approximately two million workers were missing from Britain's workforce. The government needed to act quickly to fill these gaps. A huge propaganda campaign aimed at women asked for their help with the war effort through either voluntary organisations or paid employment. Women soon began to find work in areas that they had been excluded from before.

Organisations women joined during the First World War

- **Voluntary Aid Detachment (VADs)**

Volunteer nurses, working on the Western Front, helping injured soldiers.

- **Women's Auxiliary Corps (WAAC)**

Women's army unit. Undertook administrative and clerical duties in the army, replacing men so that they were able to fight. They also acted as cooks and drivers.

- **Women's Royal Naval Service (WRNS) and Women's Royal Air force (WRAF)**

These organisations had a similar role to the WAACs but they worked for the Navy and Air Force instead.

- **Women's Land Army**

Women who worked on the farms, cultivating the land and growing crops and food. They became known as Land Girls.

SOURCE A

How will you answer your children when they ask what you did for the First World War? I must admit, although my heart was bursting with patriotism, there was a thrill and adventure that I was about to face things that were completely new to me. I was going to put myself to the test as to whether I was fit to serve my country from the point of view of intelligence. My work would entail handling a machine, and I feared anything to do with machinery.

Monica Cosens, who worked in a munitions factory during the First World War.

SOURCE B

Women working in a munitions factory in May 1917. They are doing skilled precision machine work.

SOURCE C

We went on duty at 7.30 am and came off at 8 pm, including three hours off and a weekly half day.

Vera Brittain, a nurse in France during the First World War.

SOURCE D

Women air mechanics of the Women's Royal Air Force (WRAF), established in 1918.

SOURCE E

The work women are doing is not repetitive. It demands little or no manipulative ability. It taxes the intelligence of the operatives to a high degree. Yet the work turned out has a high pitch of excellence.

From a trade journal, *The Engineer*, 20 August 1915.

SOURCE F

The first dressing I assisted was to a gangrenous leg wound, slimy and green and scarlet with the bone laid bare. It turned me sick and faint for a moment.

Vera Brittain writing about her experiences as a nurse during the First World War.

SOURCE G

Land girls on a farm in Surrey, April 1917.

SOURCE H

London has not yet grown accustomed to its policewomen. I saw one today at the corner of Whitehall, and she appeared conscious of the attention she was attracting. Physically the women are not of the type you would expect and they seem little fitted to face the hurly-burly of a street fight.

From a newspaper report of May 1915, describing public reactions to women members of the police force.

TASKS...

1 Look back to the problems that the government minister faced during the First World War (page 211). Copy the chart below to show how women helped to solve each problem.

Problem	How women helped the war effort	Skills required
How to help the injured soldiers on the battlefield.		
How to free men from clerical jobs so they can fight.		
How to provide more food for the British people.		
How to provide more munitions on the Western Front.		
How to keep life on the Home Front as organised and calm as possible.		

2 What do you think was the most important job women did to contribute to the war effort? Give reasons for your answer.

What was the impact of the Second World War on women?

Throughout the Second World War, British civilians were in constant danger from air raids, invasion and food shortages. When men were conscripted into the army, the government turned its attention towards women – as it had done during the First World War.

Ministers stressed the importance of women's roles as the main line of defence on the Home Front. A huge propaganda campaign was aimed at British women. Work was always glamorised, so that women would eagerly volunteer to help with the war effort.

Women working in a gas mask factory during the Second World War.

Working in factories is not fun. To be shut in for hours on end without even a window to see daylight was grim. The noise was terrific and at night when you shut your eyes to sleep all the noise would start again in your head. Night shifts were the worst. The work was very often monotonous. I think boredom was our worst enemy.

One woman describes her experiences of working in a factory in 1942.

A friend of mine was caught in the blast from a nearby bomb and was taken to hospital with several shrapnel wounds. The all-clear [a signal to say that the enemy attack was over] went at about 6am and we were able to go home to bed. Two hours later, I got up and went to work.

Doreen Ellis, writing in her diary about life during the Second World War.

The men were lying in such a variety of positions, often with their limbs stuck out at queer angles in the plaster splints or sometimes slung on frames and hung with weights and pulleys. The light caught the glass flasks of blood, which was still slowly dripping Into four bed cases.

Lena K. Chivers, a nurse at a casualty clearing station, August 1944.

I used to go shopping for my mother. This could sometimes take a whole morning even though the shops were just round the corner. Most of the time was spent queuing – especially for bread and meat. My mother and her friends queued for hours.

A woman recalls how rationing affected her family during the war.

Women servicing a six-ton truck during the Second World War.

A poster calling for women to join the Women's Land Army.

My white tender hands were a thing of the past. Instead, they became rough and callused. I rolled into bed at the end of the day to lay like a stone statue not daring to move in case the pounding backache transferred itself all around my aching body.

A woman called Ivy, talking about life in the Land Army.

SOURCE Q

In a large farm in Lincolnshire we worked for twelve hours a day at very hard and monotonous work and received no training. Wages were 28 shillings (£1.40) a week, out of which we had to pay £1 for our lodgings. At a smaller farm in Huntingdon, where we were expected to be trained in tractor driving, we were made to do odd jobs, including kitchen work for the farmer's wife. The farmer gave us no training and refused to pay us any wages.

One woman's description of her work as a Land Girl in 1941.

SOURCE R

British women often give orders to men. The men obey smartly and know it is no shame. For British women have proved themselves in this war. They have stuck to their posts near burning ammunition dumps, delivered messages afoot after their motorcycles have been blasted from under them. They have pulled pilots from burning planes. They have died at their gun-posts, and as they fell another girl has stepped directly into the position and 'carried on'. There isn't a single record of any British woman in uniformed service quitting her post, or failing in her duty under fire. When you see a girl in uniform with a bit of ribbon on her tunic, remember that she didn't get it for knitting more socks than anyone else.

An extract from a booklet issued by the US War Department to every US soldier entering Britain during the Second World War.

TASKS...

1 Copy and complete the chart below.

Sources which glamorise women's work	Sources which show the reality of women's work

2 Look at Sources I to R. Place the letter of each source in the correct column, to show which sources glamorise women's work and which show the reality.

3 Take an example from each column of your chart. Explain how each source either glamorises women's work or shows the reality of it.

4 You are now in a position to judge how warfare changed the position of British women in the twentieth century. Copy the diagram below into your book. You should write down key points about women's roles during both the First and Second World Wars on your diagram.

- Any similarities between women's roles should be written down in the overlapping section of the two circles.
- The differences should be listed in the correct circle.

First World War

Second World War

5 Read the statements below.

- The First and Second World Wars had no impact at all on women's lives.
- The First World War had a small impact on women's lives, but it was not until the Second World War that women's lives really changed.
- Both wars had a huge and lasting impact on women's lives.

Which statement do you support? Explain your decision.

Plenary

 SOURCE (S)

Nature doth show women to be weak, frail, impatient, feeble and foolish. For a woman to have rule or power over a kingdom, nation or city is against nature and God's revealed will.

John Knox, a sixteenth-century Scottish preacher.

 SOURCE (T)

Modern British female soldier in action in Iraq, 2003.

How might women and men in twenty-first century Britain challenge John Knox's comment?

Are there any places in the world where women might still be treated and seen as second class citizens? Where do you think these places are? Why do you think women are still treated like this in these places?

THE CHANGING NATURE OF WARFARE IN THE TWENTIETH CENTURY: CONCLUSIONS

A local museum is creating an exhibition with the title 'The Changing nature of warfare in the twentieth century'. You have been asked to submit proposals to the museum on what should be included in the exhibition. You have six exhibits you can include. These can be photographs, paintings, drawings, artefacts and written sources. For each exhibit you include you must add a commentary explanation of what the exhibit shows and why it has been included in the exhibition – its importance. Think about what it would tell visitors about the changing nature of warfare in the twentieth century.

Your exhibits must cover the whole of the twentieth century not just concentrate on one aspect, for example the First World War.

Complete this exercise on a larger copy of this exhibit sheet:

Exhibit	Why should this be included in the exhibition?	Explain what it shows and why it is important in explaining the changing nature of warfare in the twentieth century.

Index